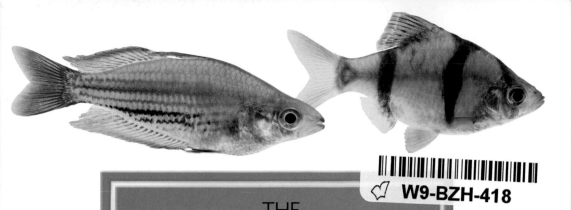

THE

~~TROPICAL~~

#524   03-05-2015 11:27AM

CONTENTS – *Practical Sections*

First edition for the United States
and Canada published in 2005 by
Barron's Educational Series, Inc.

First published in 2004 by Interpet
Publishing

International Standard Book No.:
0-7641-2986-4

Library of Congress Catalog
Card No.: 2004096276

Printed in China

9 8 7 6 5 4 3 2 1

Part One: Setting up the aquarium 6-41

Part Two: Options and continuing care *42-77*

Author

Gina Sandford's interest in fishkeeping began with a goldfish and developed to include sticklebacks, young perch, pike and eventually tropical fish. She has kept and bred many species but has a particular interest in catfishes. She has written several books and contributed many articles to magazines and journals.

Other contributors:
Peter Hiscock
Stuart Thraves
Nick Fletcher
Derek Lambert

CONTENTS – *Fish Profiles*

PART ONE

Setting up the aquarium

The thought of putting together an aquarium can be daunting. The first part of this book shows you how to set up a tropical freshwater aquarium. Read it through and then start again at the beginning. What equipment do you need? Where do you put it? How does it all fit together? Where do you buy it?

Finding a reliable aquatic retailer is the key. This may be a single shop or a large pet store chain. Look around several before you pick one that appeals to you. Listen to the advice you are offered and look at the health of the livestock. See how long people stay in the shop; fishkeepers are notorious for spending several hours in a good establishment, looking around and chatting with the staff.

Now, put aside those fears that you are going to be thought of as a complete idiot; everyone has to start somewhere and a good aquatic dealer will know this. He or she will be well aware that novices are potential customers for a long time if they are treated properly and helped along the way. The best time to visit the shop to talk about your needs is when it is quiet, say during the week or when it first opens in the morning. At a busy weekend, the retailer may advise you to return when he can spend time with you. This is a good sign. Similarly, when you come to buy your tropical freshwater fish, do not be put off if the retailer will not sell you a particular species because it grows too large, has a bad temper, will not agree with your other fish or is difficult to feed.

Your next task will be to put your purchases together to create your aquarium. Over the next pages we will take you through the process step by step. Take your time over this. The aim is to complete each step successfully so that by the end you will have a fully working aquarium to house and display tropical freshwater fish and plants in a healthy and attractive environment that will be with you for years ahead. You will soon become a dedicated fishkeeper.

Choosing a tank and stand

Tank and stand or cabinet styles are very much a matter of personal taste, and there is a wide range of designs to choose from. Your main considerations should be the available space in your home, how much you want to spend, the number and size of fish you want to keep (which in turn will be governed by surface area), and how you are going to transport the tank and stand home.

Tanks are normally rectangular and constructed of glass sheets bonded together with silicone sealant. Retailers carry the standard sizes, but customized sizes can be made to order. If you take this route, remember that your cabinet or stand will also need to be custom-made. Some tanks are supplied with hoods. They are either the standard shape that we will demonstrate in this book or they are molded to fit a particular tank. The choice is yours.

Good-quality aquatic outlets will advise on the best choices within your price range, and many will offer to deliver bulky items that will not fit into your car, but some may charge for this extra service.

Acrylic tanks

Acrylic tanks are usually more expensive but are becoming a popular alternative to glass. They are a great improvement on the old-style plastic aquariums that scratched and stained easily.

Above: *The trim at the top of the tank should match the color of the stand and hood to help create a complete unit, rather than something that has been thrown together. Using black baseboard as a shelf at the bottom also helps to complete the picture.*

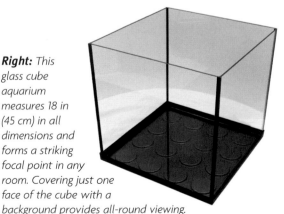

Right: *This glass cube aquarium measures 18 in (45 cm) in all dimensions and forms a striking focal point in any room. Covering just one face of the cube with a background provides all-round viewing.*

Below: Tanks and cabinets such as these are designed as pieces of furniture and you can order a veneer to match your decor. The hood is part of the unit, as are sliding glass trays that form an effective condensation tray and give access to the tank. There is a shelf for the light to rest on and space at the rear of the hood for the lighting unit. Cutouts at the back allow for cables, air lines and filter pipes.

Left: Flat-packed or ready-made cabinets are usually available in a choice of finishes. Some have cupboards below them in which you can safely and tidily conceal lighting units, external filters, and cables.

Sizes and capacities of standard tanks

Tank	Volume	Weight of water
24x12x12 in (60x30x30 cm)	12 gal (55 liters)	120 lb (55 kg)
24x12x15 in (60x30x38 cm)	15 gal (68 liters)	150 lb (68 kg)
36x12x12 in (90x30x30 cm)	18 gal (82 liters)	180 lb (82 kg)
36x12x15 in (90x30x38 cm)	23 gal (104 liters)	230 lb (104 kg)
48x12x12 in (120x30x30 cm)	24 gal (109 liters)	240 lb (109 kg)
48x12x15 in (120x30x38 cm)	30 gal (136 liters)	300 lb (136 kg)

Above: Fishkeepers today have a wide choice of aquarium shapes and sizes. This curved tank on a purpose-built stand is supplied with lighting and filtration equipment.

Siting the tank

**Finding the best position
for the aquarium**

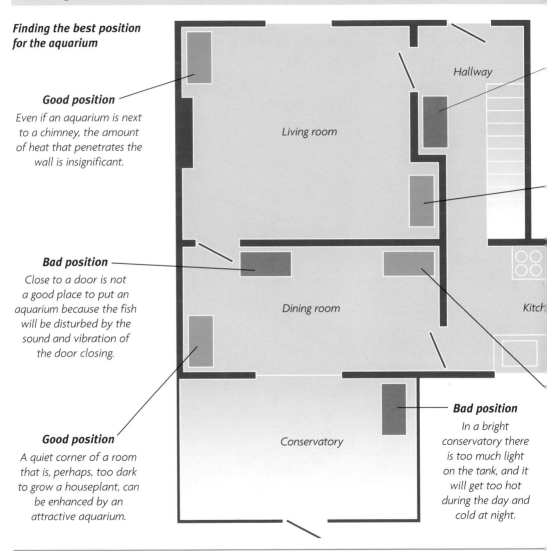

Good position

Even if an aquarium is next
to a chimney, the amount
of heat that penetrates the
wall is insignificant.

Bad position

Close to a door is not
a good place to put an
aquarium because the fish
will be disturbed by the
sound and vibration of
the door closing.

Good position

A quiet corner of a room
that is, perhaps, too dark
to grow a houseplant, can
be enhanced by an
attractive aquarium.

Bad position

In a bright
conservatory there
is too much light
on the tank, and it
will get too hot
during the day and
cold at night.

Hallway

Living room

Dining room

Kitch

Conservatory

Bad position

Although an aquarium makes a nice feature in a hallway, it is not the best place because of drafts caused when the door is open and closed, and disturbance caused by passing traffic.

Good position

Choose a quiet area, such as an alcove, provided you have access to service the tank and to an electricity supply.

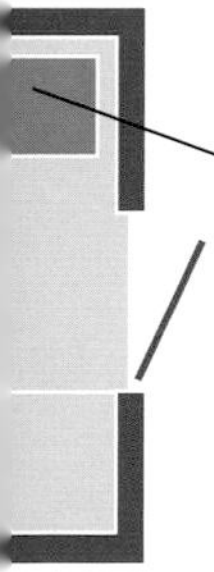

Bad position

Putting an aquarium in a kitchen is not a good idea because fumes from cooking may affect the fish.

Good position

In this position, the tank is far enough away from the doors not to be affected by people passing by.

The position of the tank in the room is often a compromise, since it is rare to find the optimum conditions. Bear in mind that fully set up tanks are extremely heavy. Since 1 gallon of water weighs 10 lb (1 liter weighs 1 kg) and the 24x12x15 in (60x30x38 cm) tank featured in this book holds about 15 gal (68 liters), you can see that it will weigh 150 lb (68 kg) without the weight of the tank itself, cabinet, rocks, gravel, etc. A concrete floor should pose no problems, but on floorboards, try to position the stand as shown below. This is even more important for the larger-sized tanks. Consider the proximity of power points. Site the tank so that it is stable and will not fall onto anything or anyone. There should be no risk of anyone falling over the tank or the electricity supply to it.

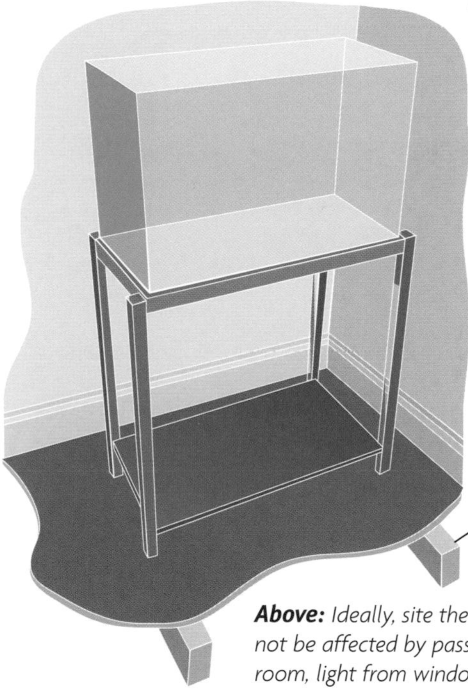

If you can, position the stand so that the weight of the finished unit is taken by the joists and not the floorboards.

Above: *Ideally, site the unit where it will not be affected by passing traffic through the room, light from windows, and heat from radiators. Pick a secluded corner where you can easily install and service the aquarium.*

11

Installing the tank

To demonstrate setting up an aquarium, we have chosen a standard-sized tank measuring 24x12x15 in high (60x30x38 cm). If you are just starting out in fishkeeping, this size of aquarium is ideal. It is compact enough for you to set up easily and will fit into a small house or apartment or, if you are a younger fishkeeper, in your bedroom if that is the only place available to you. Although relatively small, this size of aquarium does hold enough water to prevent any rapid fluctuations in water conditions such as temperature and pH (degree of acidity or alkalinity). Any changes that do take place will happen gradually, thus preventing any great degree of stress on your fish. It also gives you time to carry out whatever measures are necessary to alleviate the situation before it becomes a disaster, such as replacing a heater that has failed.

Having checked that your stand or cabinet is level, make sure that when the tank is in position, the whole unit is still level, both from side to side and back to front. If necessary, make any minor adjustments, but ask someone to hold the tank so that there is no danger of it falling on you.

Checklist

These are the items you will need for installation:

Tank and hood (may be an integral unit)
Stand or cabinet
Mallet
Baseboard for use on the stand
Polystyrene tiles

Level
Scissors
Craft knife
Screwdrivers
Pliers
Cable clips or ties
Adhesive tape
Insulation tape
Water jug
Nail brush
Copious supplies of tea or coffee

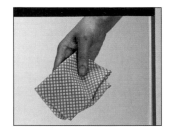

Your next task is to clean the tank. It may look perfectly clean, but there is bound to be a fine film of dust inside it, which, if left where it is, will appear as a film on the water surface of the finished aquarium. Use a new cloth and water only to clean the tank, as any detergent can be lethal to livestock.

It is worth filling the tank at this point to check for leaks – a very rare occurrence these days, but a problem that is easy to fix now. If it leaks, drain it down and consult your dealer, who should replace it. If the tank is secondhand, drain it down, dry it and reseal it with silicone aquarium sealer.

Setting up the stand

Above: Stands usually have feet that you can adjust by screwing them either up or down. Cabinets may require some packing under one edge to achieve the right level. In such a case, always make sure that what you use is safe.

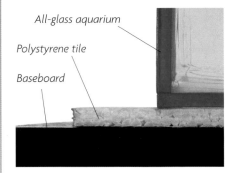

All-glass aquarium

Polystyrene tile

Baseboard

Above: Always seat glass tanks on a layer of polystyrene to even out imperfections in the baseboard. Even a tiny piece of grit can cause a fine fracture in the base glass once the tank is full of water and gravel.

Choosing and preparing substrates

Up to a point, the choice of substrate is a matter of taste, but you must also meet the needs of the fish you are going to keep and the type of filtration used.

Natural sand and gravel are available in various grades. The best types have rounded grains and are lime free. (Gravels that originate from offshore sites may contain shell fragments, and these can harden the water.) Some fish like to bury in the substrate and others feed by sifting through it. In this case, river sand, or fine or medium gravels are suitable.

Another consideration is the type of filtration you are intending to use. Sand and fine gravel are too small for use with undergravel filters, as the grains fall into the slats in the filter plates and block them. Coarse gravel can be used with larger fish species but needs care, because it is easy for debris and uneaten food to become trapped in the gaps between the grains.

Colored gravels are also available. Only buy them from a reliable aquatic outlet, because in the past, dyes have been known to leach from some colored gravels, and these have proved fatal to fish.

River sand

Having rounded grains, river sand makes an excellent choice if you are keeping bottom-dwelling species. It is a non-compacting sand that allows the free passage of water and plant roots.

Coarse gravel

You can use coarse gravel in large setups or mix it with medium gravel for a different effect. It is especially useful for creating a stream-bed effect in the tank.

Medium gravel

This is the standard gravel of the trade, and it provides a suitable substrate for just about any size of aquarium.

Fine gravel

This is a good choice for a smaller aquarium where medium or coarse gravel would look out of proportion.

If you are using an undergravel filter, fit it to the base of the tank before you add the gravel.

As you add the gravel, you can spread it over the base. Some people like to keep the substrate flat, others like to bank it slightly so that it is lower at the front than the back. The choice is yours, but remember that it should be deep enough to put your plants in.

Adding the gravel

Sand and gravel are dirty. Although washed before they leave the quarry, they are still dusty and must be washed thoroughly before use. Place small amounts in a bucket, add water and agitate it, using your hands or, say, a wooden spoon kept for the purpose. Drain and repeat as necessary until the water drains clear. Repeat until all your substrate is cleaned.

How much gravel?

With an undergravel filter, the substrate should be about 2.4 in (6 cm) deep, arranged evenly. If you are not using an undergravel filter, it should be 1.6-2 in (4-5 cm) deep.

Installing an internal power filter

There are two basic types of power filter: internal and external, and, as the names suggest, they are sited either in the aquarium or outside it. Fortunately for us, they both work on the same principal of taking in water, passing it through the filter medium, and returning it to the aquarium. Movement of the water is generated by an electrical motor driving an impeller. The filter medium provides a large area that beneficial bacteria can colonize. They break down much of the waste matter produced by the fish (see the nitrogen cycle, page 26). Other materials, such as activated carbon, can be incorporated to remove other toxic substances.

Right: Internal power filters are suitable for the smaller aquarium. The foam insert is colonized with bacteria. When servicing the tank, rinse the foam with tank water (removed when doing the water change). This way, you remove fine, clogging debris but retain the beneficial bacteria in the foam.

The venturi effect

As water is pumped back into the tank, it can also be aerated by a venturi pipe. This accelerates the water flow and draws in a stream of air from above the surface.

Back-up aeration

Although a power filter provides aeration, it is a good idea to have an air pump and air stone to provide backup aeration in case of filter failure.

Internal filter

A submersible pump provides the power source. It may or may not have a venturi to aerate the water (see above).

The foam cartridge houses the beneficial bacteria.

The plastic barrel has an internal divider to allow good water flow. This complete unit pushes onto the pump.

Position the filter with the nozzle facing outward. Direct the outflow across the diagonal of the aquarium.

Safety first

Never run the filter pump without water in the tank, as it will burn out. If you want to test it, submerge it in a bucket of water.

Fixing the cradle

Unpack your filter and read the manufacturer's instructions carefully, as different models vary slightly. Assemble the filter as instructed. Attach the suckers supplied to the outside of the filter or carrying frame. You may need to wet them to get them to stick to the glass.

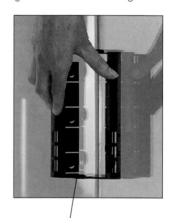

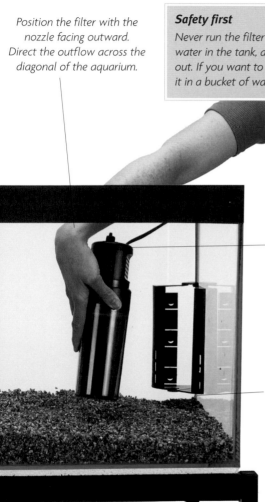

Check the manufacturer's instructions, and position the filter head at or just below the water surface.

Allow a gap between the base of the filter and the substrate to avoid the accumulation of dirt and debris and to allow free passage of water into and around the filter canister.

Carrying frames make removing the filter unit easy for cleaning and maintenance.

Note: You may wish to use an external filter for your tank. See pages 44-45 for the options of using a canister or hang-on external power filter.

Heating the water

Tropical fish and plants require warmth to keep them alive. Outside their preferred range, their bodies cease to function properly and they die. The temperature of the water also affects its oxygen-holding capacity; the warmer the water, the less oxygen it can hold, and species that are not accustomed to lower oxygen levels will be seen gasping at the surface. In cooler conditions, the fish tend to slow down and rest near the bottom. Plants may put on a spurt of growth and become straggly or they may disintegrate. Fortunately, with modern technology, maintaining the water at a natural level of 73-75°F (23-24°C) is quite easy to accomplish by using one of the heating units available from your local aquarium dealer. Now, you may think that in a centrally heated home you do not need a heater – not so! During the day, the ambient room temperature may keep the aquarium water just warm enough. However, it will not raise the water temperature to that of the room; the water will be several degrees lower than the room temperature. So, what happens during the night when the heating is turned down while you are asleep? The tank temperature drops, perhaps to critical or even fatal levels. Therefore, you need to provide the correct temperature range, and a heater-thermostat will accomplish this.

> **Safety first**
> Never turn on the heater until the tank is full of water.

Most manufacturers recommend placing the heater at an angle (heating element at the bottom) so that, as the heat rises, it does not go straight past the thermostat.

Installing the heater

Unpack the heater-thermostat and keep the instructions that tell you how to position and adjust it. Read these carefully, as there may be variations between manufacturers. Attach the suckers. Check to see what temperature it is set at and adjust if necessary.

Leave a small gap between the bottom of the heater and the substrate. Do not cover units with substrate, as they will overheat. Make sure the water flow is not obstructed by any tank decorations placed in front of the heater.

Above: *The suckers are usually supplied detached from the unit. Place them over the heater and slide them along so that one is near the top and the other near the bottom. You may need to wet them to stick them to the glass. Always keep spare suckers and a spare heater-thermostat in stock.*

Types of heater

The combined submersible heater-thermostat is the ideal choice for the novice fishkeeper. It is easy to regulate and, being submersible, cannot be easily tampered with once set at the desired temperature. Separate heaters are also available in the form of submersible heaters or undertank heating mats. Both are controlled by either external or internal thermostats. (Children love twiddling the knobs on an external thermostat, so be careful where you site them!) There are also power filters on the market that incorporate a heating unit in the system.

As the water is circulated by the filter, it will pass the heater and warm up.

What size heater? The size of heater you need (wattage) will depend on the size of your aquarium. As a guide, you need 50 watts per 6 gallons (27 liters) of water.

Right: *Combined heater-thermostats are easy to adjust by turning the knob at the top until you reach the desired temperature. Models are available calibrated in °F or °C or both scales side by side. Some units have a light to indicate whether they are on or off. Make sure you can see this.*

Choosing and preparing wood

Wood can be very useful in the aquarium, not only physically pleasing to look at, but also forming an important part in the diet of some fish. It has a much softer look than rocks, both in shape and texture. Bogwood and mopani are featured here and should be available from your local aquatic outlet. Vine roots may also be available. Do not be tempted to collect wood from the wild, as you can never be sure what you are collecting; beetles like to use dead timber, and the thought of beetles and their grubs appearing in your tank is not a pleasant one!

Wood is dusty and dirty, but it will have been washed before you buy it. However, you should check it over and remove any dead bits of moss or fine roots that may be sticking to it. Most of this can be done with a dry brush but you may need to wash and scrub it over. You may need to soak larger pieces of wood in a bucket (or, if they are very large, the bathtub!) to release some of the tannins that will stain the water. Change the water every day or so until the staining is at an acceptable level (carbon in the filter will help reduce some of this in the aquarium).

It is often thought that varnishing bogwood will prevent tannins leaching into the water. However, bogwood is a natural substance with many nooks and crannies that are impossible to penetrate with varnish. Water does manage to get into these crevices and can lift the varnish, rendering it useless. The other problem arises with fish that eat bogwood as part of their diet or rasp on it to create breeding hollows, such as bristlenose catfish. Varnishing is only practical with smooth-surfaced wood, such as bamboo (see page 46).

You can position wood in front of the heater, but make sure it does not rest against it. Take care not to knock and break the heater when putting it in place. The wood is not only part of the aquarium decor, it also serves a practical function by concealing the heater.

For details of synthetic wood see pages 48-49

Adding the wood

Put the wood in place and bed it down well into the substrate to ensure that it does not fall over. Position it so that it will not disrupt access to equipment that may need to be replaced or serviced. If you find that the wood will not quite fit your tank, try to break it carefully, rather than cut it with a saw. Look at the wood and be guided by its shape and graining; if it looks like a tree root coming down into the tank, use it as such. If it is more like a fallen branch, it may be best to lay it down in the tank. At this stage, with no water in the tank, you can play around with it easily.

Bogwood is the standard wood for the aquarium. It requires more cleaning and soaking than other woods.

Mopani costs more than bogwood because it has been sand blasted to clean it, which also gives it a lighter color.

Left: A stiff-bristled nail brush or scrubbing brush will dislodge dirt and debris from the nooks and crannies in wood. Brush off as much as possible from the dry wood. You may have to wet the wood to remove stubborn marks.

Do not place any wood in front of the filter or you will obstruct the water flow. It is worth checking that your piece of wood sinks before you put it in the tank; some have been known to float!

Do not collect your own waterlogged wood

However tempting it may be, do not collect waterlogged wood ("bogwood") from the wild. In many places, such wood may be contaminated with industrial chemicals, pesticides, and fertilizers that will leach out into the tank and prove toxic to your fish.

Always buy wood from an aquatic retailer or pet store. These pieces are safe for use in an aquarium, and although they will need soaking to release tannins, they will not harm your livestock. Never take chances with your valuable and delicate fishes.

Choosing and cleaning rocks

Bear in mind that waterworn rocks look much more natural than broken, angular pieces and try to stick to one type of rock rather than mix different colors and textures. If you want to build up a rocky structure in the aquarium, glue together cleaned, dry rocks with silicone sealant before putting them in the tank. This will prevent rock structures from falling down.

Below: *The rocks shown here are all suitable for a general community aquarium. They are inert (which means they will not leach anything nasty into the water) and hard enough to provide spawning sites for fish should they wish to use them.*

A rock dropped from a sufficient height could crack the tank. Hold it securely as you place it in the tank.

Rocks in shades of green and gray increase the range of color available.

Weathered rock has natural fissures that create interesting textures in the aquarium.

The dark tones of slate provide dramatic contrast.

Warm colors glow in the tank lights.

The grainy texture and solidity of granite add "weight" to tank displays.

Right: *Rocks need washing – indeed they need scrubbing! The amount of dirt that can stick to a seemingly clean rock is amazing, especially if the piece has deep crevices, such as this piece of weathered rock. Be sure to remove all dust, dirt, and pieces of moss or lichens to prevent them fouling your tank.*

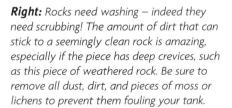

Unsuitable rocks

Avoid rocks that will change your water chemistry such as tufa and limestone, which will make the water hard and alkaline. Also some attractively colored rocks, particularly from western North America, contain metal ores that can leach substances into the water that are toxic to fish at very low concentrations.

Be careful when adding heavy rocks that you do not accidentally damage the equipment you have just installed.

Positioning the rocks

1 Carefully plan where you are going to place your rocks. They are heavy, and you may need help to lift and position large pieces. Wriggle them down into the substrate until they are seated on the base glass to prevent fish from undermining them.

2 When you are satisfied with the position of the main piece(s), you can add the smaller ones until you have completed your layout. Remember to leave enough room to replace or service any equipment in the aquarium and avoid disrupting the water flow from the filter.

Left: Smaller waterworn pebbles can help to take the edge off larger angular rocks.

Safe rocks to use

For a basic community aquarium, it is vital to choose inert rocks that will not affect the water chemistry or contaminate the tank. Safe rocks include granite, slate, washed coal, basalt, flint, sandstone, quartz, and lava rock. To be sure, buy rocks for the aquarium from an aquatic retailer or pet store and wash them well before use.

Adding the water

Filling the tank

The easiest way to fill your tank is with a jug. At this stage you can use cold or warm water, as no livestock or plants are present. Gently pour the water over a flat stone to avoid disturbing the substrate too much. It takes time but is better than destroying your aquarium decor. If you have no suitable stones in your setup, pour the water into a saucer.

Use a clean jug to start filling the tank. As the water level rises, you can add the water by slowly pouring from a bucket, checking that it is not disturbing the substrate too much.

The more you clean the gravel before you put it in the aquarium, the less likely it is to cause cloudiness as you add the water. Once the aquarium is full, carefully rearrange any substrate you have disturbed by over-vigorous pouring.

Tap water

The water provided by your local water company is treated to render it fit for human consumption. Chlorine gas is commonly used for purification and if it has been heavily used, you will smell it when you draw water from your tap. If you allow the water to stand for 24 hours, the chlorine will disperse. You can speed up the process by using an airstone to agitate the water.

Another chemical added by water companies is chloramine. This is more difficult to deal with, as it does not disperse naturally. You will need to buy a water conditioner to neutralize it. (This will also deal with the chlorine.) Check with your water company to see what they add to your water. They should also let you know if they are intending to flush the mains with anything to kill bugs, etc. that may affect fish.

In areas with naturally soft tap water, copper contamination from newly installed copper pipes can cause problems for fish and plants. Chemically active filter media, such as PolyBio Marine's PolyFilter©, will remove copper from the water, turning blue-green as it does so.

Tank hygiene

If you use a bucket, make sure that it is free from any residues of cleaning products. It is far better to keep a bucket solely for aquarium use.

Above: Using a tapwater conditioner is a quick and reliable method of neutralizing the chemicals added to make the water suitable for human consumption. It is then safe to use in the aquarium.

The pH scale

The pH scale is used to determine the acidity or alkalinity of the water. It runs from 0 (extremely acidic) to 14 (extremely alkaline), with 7 being termed neutral. It is a logarithmic scale, each step being 10 times the previous one. This is why seemingly small changes can have dramatic effects. Test kits and electronic meters are available to measure pH.

Running in the system before adding plants

How the nitrogen cycle works

While we are waiting for the system to be ready for us to add the first plants, we should explore some natural chemical processes that take place within an aquarium. The most important of these is the circulation of nitrogen-containing compounds, commonly known as the nitrogen cycle. This natural process is the means by which dead and decaying waste products containing nitrogen are converted by bacteria from poisonous compounds, such as ammonia, into harmless substances, such as nitrates, that are then taken up by the plants. It will start happening in your tank as soon as you set it up, and the filtration system will help it along. As the filtration system becomes colonized by helpful bacteria, it becomes more efficient. However, as soon as you add fish, there is a system overload, and it takes a few days for the numbers of bacteria to build up to cope with the extra waste. This is why it is best to add a few fish at a time and not all of them at once. The first thing to happen is that bacteria break down the toxic ammonia excreted by fish and produced by decomposition. This is converted to nitrites, which are also toxic to fish at very low concentrations. Nitrites are converted by bacteria to much less harmful nitrates. In an ideal world, all the nitrates would be taken up by the plants, but in an aquarium, it is not that simple! We usually overload our tanks with fish that produce too much waste for the plants to use. The result is high nitrate levels. To remove these, carry out regular partial water changes.

Ammonia is excreted by fish through the gills and in their waste products.

Nitrates are taken up by the plants as a fertilizer.

Ammonia (extremely toxic) is converted to nitrites by bacteria in the filtration system.

Nitrites (also toxic at low concentrations) are converted to nitrates by bacteria in the filtration system.

Safety first

Make sure that all the equipment is properly installed (submersed to the correct levels and firmly attached) before switching on the power supply.

Make sure the heater-thermostat is submerged.

Any cloudiness in the water should be removed by the filtration system.

Oxygen and carbon dioxide levels

Oxygen (and other gases) enter and leave the water at the surface. Oxygen levels can be boosted by agitating the water surface by using an airstone or the spray bar return from a power filter. It is important to remember that the oxygen-carrying capacity of water decreases as the temperature rises. Dissolved carbon dioxide levels can affect fish-carrying capacity but excess amounts can be readily removed by aeration.

Check that the filter system is working, and adjust the direction and rate of flow if necessary.

Planting up the aquarium

Plants play a vital role in a well-balanced aquarium, because they help to lower nitrate levels (see page 26). Choose aquatic plants, rather than the houseplants that are sometimes sold for aquariums.

Select plants by size, leaf shape, and color. Use tall ones for the back of the aquarium, medium and short ones for the center and front. Plants are sold either potted or bare rooted. Both are fine, provided the plants look healthy (see page 33).

Put in each plant individually; it seems fussy but is well worthwhile. (After all, you would not plant cabbages or roses three or four to a hole and expect them all to grow into healthy plants.) Allow enough space between the plants for the light to reach the substrate. Plant in rows and stagger the rows so that the whole grouping looks like a wall of plants from the front.

Safety first
Switch off all electrical equipment before starting work on the aquarium. As an extra precaution, also unplug it from the main outlet.

This healthy bacopa is growing in a planting medium contained in a small plastic basket.

It is especially important that cryptocorynes do not have badly damaged leaves, as these quickly rot back to the crown.

Left: *Unraveled from its potting medium, this cryptocoryne reveals that it is made up of several small plants. Giving each plant its own space to grow creates a carpet of plants in the aquarium.*

For details of other suitable plants see pages 50-57

Before you start planting, drop the water level slightly. This not only stops you splashing water, but also saves you getting your sleeves wet!

Place the next plant about 0.8 in (2 cm) away from the first. Continue like this until you have a row of the required length along the back of the tank.

Repeat the process for the next row about 0.8 in (2 cm) in front of the first, placing the plants in front of the spaces in the row behind. Repeat as necessary to make more rows or partial rows.

Planting vallisneria

Gently hold the plant near the base and, using a finger of the same hand, make a hole in the gravel. This prevents the stem and roots bruising as you slide the plant into the substrate, just deep enough to prevent it coming loose. This takes a little practice, but persevere.

Start by planting a row at the back of the aquarium and work forward. Planting depth is dictated by the type of plant. In this case, look at the white area at the base of the plant; the top of the white area should be at the surface.

Planting up the aquarium

Some plants are sold as cuttings. They are sold loose, in bunches, or potted. Whichever is available to you, apply the same rules. Look for healthy plants with good green leaves and no dead or dying leaves or stems. Cuttings are particularly prone to rotting at the base because the stems are damaged when they are thrust into the gravel. This is even more likely when they are gathered in a clump and held together with a metal strip, which bruises the stems, creating a site of infection.

These plants have a great advantage in the aquarium: you can cut them to the required length to create your desired design. They naturally grow quite tall and may be used toward the rear of the aquarium, but they can also be cut to shorter lengths so that each row is slightly shorter than the one behind, thus creating a wall of plants.

Left: Carefully remove the metal strip from the base of the cabombas and gently separate each cutting. Take your time. Cabomba is a delicate plant that bruises easily.

Left: Using a pair of sharp scissors, cut away the bare, damaged stem just below a leaf joint and discard the damaged portion. If you need shorter plants, you can cut further up the stem.

Hints and tips

When you get your plants home, unpack them carefully. Once prepared for planting, lay them out on a tray in shallow, warm water to prevent them drying out. If necessary, cover them with a plastic bag.

Allow yourself plenty of time to plant up the aquarium. Rushing the process can damage the plants.

If you cannot find all the plants you want in one go, do not panic; you can always add one or two later on.

Aquarium plants sold as cuttings

The main plants available as cuttings are the bacopas, cabombas, hygrophilas, ludwigias, and water wisteria. Treat all these, and any other cuttings you come across, as described here.

For details of other suitable plants see pages 50-57

Planting cabomba

Start planting at the rear of the tank and work toward the front, taking care not to pull out the plants that are already in place. As this tank is planted up, we are leaving an open space in the foreground so that bottom-dwelling fish can come out and feed.

Put in each plant individually. Space the plants so that their leaves just touch (it will vary from species to species) and light can reach the substrate.

Choose plants with colors and leaf shapes that complement each other. The coarse leaves of the vallisneria are ideal for concealing a filter, whereas the softer-leaved cabomba would be battered in this position. It is far better used in a quieter area to soften the edges of the wood.

Continue planting until you have created a wall of plants across the back of the aquarium, but avoid placing the cabomba in the direct flow from the filter.

Planting up the aquarium

You can use large plants, such as Amazon swordplants, to provide a focal point in the aquarium. Since they grow quite big, a single plant in a tank of this size is sufficient. However, the pygmy chain swordplant, *Echinodorus tenellus*, remains small and is suitable for the front of the tank, where it will carpet the substrate.

You can also use cryptocoryne as a spot plant, with several of the taller species planted close by and low-growing varieties as carpet plants in the mid- to foreground area. Once established, these spread by runners, and you will need to keep them in check; otherwise they will overrun the tank. These plants are available bare-rooted or potted; you may find up to six or seven cryptocoryne plantlets per pot.

Amazon swordplants have quite a large spread of leaves, which create shaded areas. These are ideal places for low-growing shade-loving species, such as some of the small cryptocorynes.

Planting Amazon swordplants

Hold the prepared plant near the base and gently push it into the substrate, using your fingers to create the hole as you push into the gravel. Make sure that the roots are buried in the substrate; otherwise the plant will float free.

Position the plant where it will be seen to full advantage and will also have room to spread its leaves. We have chosen to place it in front of the wood but behind the pebbles.

For details of other suitable plants see pages 50-57

Choosing healthy plants

Always look for healthy green leaves (or red if this is the natural color of the plant) with no signs of yellowing. Choose plants with a short distance between whorls of leaves (a lengthy space is a sign of forced growth). Avoid plants with damaged leaves (holes or tears) or falling leaves, plants with damaged crowns, and plants with damaged stems.

1 Remove the plant from its basket and gently tease away the growing medium that is usually wrapped around the base. This should reveal the base of the plant and the root system. The healthy roots are the white ones.

Continue to plant up the tank. You can conceal the edges of this rock with a thicket of ludwigia to the side and perhaps one or two small cryptocorynes between it and the pebbles. When you have finished planting, top up the tank once more.

2 Carefully remove any small pieces of growing medium attached to the roots. If the medium looks like damp paper, it will come away easily. If it resembles a blanket of coarse filter wool, it is more difficult to remove.

Preparing the hood

The hood not only covers the aquarium to prevent dust and dirt entering and fish escaping, it also houses the light source that is essential to promote healthy plant growth and allows you to see your fish. There are different styles of hood, so you may need to modify this sequence slightly for your hood. For example, in some, the lighting clips are already in place at the front of the hood. Other tanks have integral hoods and the strip light sits on a glass shelf. Make sure you know which steps you need to take to prepare your hood. Unpack it and the starter unit and check that you have everything you need.

Lighting tubes

Fluorescent tubes are now the industry standard. They have been developed in several colors to imitate daylight, promote plant growth, and enhance fish color. They can also be used in combination; for example, a white light (bottom) plus a pink light (top) covers the full spectrum and enhances the fish color. Blue is normally for marines and invertebrates. For a beginner, a good white light is the most suitable.

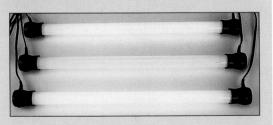

Fitting a fluorescent tube in the hood

1 *Place the starter unit into the back chamber of the hood. This unit is quite heavy, so work on a table or on the floor so that nothing accidentally falls into the tank and breaks either the tank or the equipment in it.*

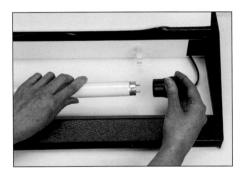

2 *Connect the tube carefully, making sure that the pins on the tube fit into the holes in the end caps. Do not cut away the black covering of the end caps to make things easier; it is there for your safety to keep water and electricity apart!*

Installing the lighting in the hood

Align the tube with the front of the clips and gently push it into position. Take care not to use so much force that you break the clips or the tube. You may need help when installing the light, as the front flap of the hood can easily fall forward onto your hands, and it is useful if someone else holds it open. It is light and does not hurt, but it is annoying when it happens.

Gently pull any excess length of flying lead back through the holes in the hood and lay them tidily in the rear chamber.

The hood is white inside, which helps to reflect light back into the aquarium.

Cable ties keep straggling leads tidy in the rear chamber.

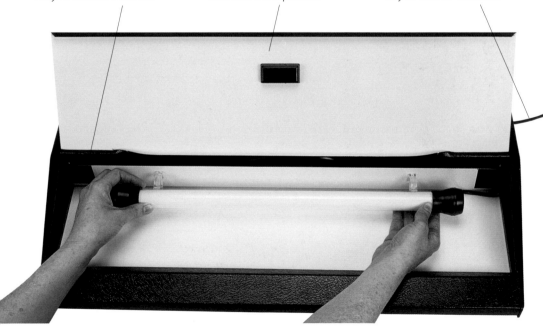

Fitting the condensation tray and hood

The condensation tray serves three purposes: it limits water loss by reducing evaporation; it prevents the small amount of evaporation from reaching the electrical fittings of the lighting unit; and it stops fish jumping out of the tank. Condensation trays can be made of plastic, as here, or glass. Sometimes it is necessary to modify the condensation tray to accommodate cables and pipes.

Some aquariums are supplied complete with glass condensation trays that slide on runners to allow easy access to the tank. Because they are made of a clear material, they allow the free passage of light into the aquarium. If this is reduced, plant growth can suffer. Make sure that the cover glass is kept clean at all times. Regularly wipe it over with a damp cloth to keep it free of algae and to remove a buildup of salts and any remnants of flake food that have been spilled when feeding your fish.

Complete hoods

You can buy hoods already fitted with a fluorescent tube as part of a complete aquarium system. The lighting unit is protected from water damage, which means that a condensation tray is not necessary.

1 *Check that wires and/or pipes can pass easily through the cutoff section. Do not forget that with this type of condensation tray you will also need to cut out a corner at the front of the tank to allow you to feed the fish.*

2 *Finally, put the modified condensation tray in place over the aquarium.*

Fitting the hood

This can be a tricky operation because the hood, complete with its light fitting, is quite heavy. If you are unsure about lifting it and placing it on the tank by yourself, ask someone to help you. It is much safer than dropping the hood into the tank! As the mains lead is trailing out of the back of the hood, either put the plug in your pocket so that you do not trip over it or coil the lead and put it out of the way in the rear chamber of the hood.

Make sure that the hood is facing the right way when you put it on the tank. The chamber housing the starter unit goes at the back of the aquarium.

As you lower the hood onto the tank, remember that the condensation tray is in place. If the hood with its heavy lighting unit slips, it can crash straight through the tray.

Just before you put on the hood, stand back and look at the tank. If necessary, make any minor adjustments to the positions of the plants and decorations.

Choosing a background and maturing the tank

Backgrounds are a matter of personal taste. The best ones are plastic and available on a roll, so they are both waterproof and easy to cut to size. If you have chosen a picture background and you need to trim it to fit the height of your tank, the design will dictate whether you trim the top or the bottom. For example, if it shows a planted aquarium, trim the bottom, otherwise you will see the cut-off tops of plants through the tank. However, if you have chosen the tree roots, the top would be the best place to cut. Choose a background that complements your tank; a solid wall of rock behind plants would look out of place. We have chosen a neutral background – black – as this adds depth to the aquarium and brings out the colors in the plants and fish.

Adding the thermometer

Position the thermometer where it is easy to read and accessible. Avoid putting it in the direct flow from the filter or it will get battered against the glass. This internal thermometer is more versatile than the stick-on form, as you can remove it to check the temperature when doing water changes. Position a stick-on thermometer where it will not be affected by sunlight falling on the tank or by the heat from nearby radiators.

Right: *A good position for the thermometer is in a front corner so that the top is just below the water surface.*

Left: *Attach the background to the back of the tank on the outside. Secure it with clear adhesive tape along the entire length of each side. This is sufficient for a tank of this size, but on wider tanks you may need more tape along the top and bottom as well. You may need someone to help you with this.*

This roll has a black background on one side and blue on the other. The blue grades from light to dark across its width. Both provide a neutral background.

Maturing the tank

Switch on all the equipment and check that it is working. Remember that fish tanks need time to mature. Total maturation of the filtration system takes about 36 days, but you could add the first few fish after 7-10 days and a few more a week or so later. This way, you build up your full complement of fish over a five- to six-week period or even longer.

The lighting should be running for up to 14 hours a day to promote healthy plant growth. The best way to achieve this is to use a timer that automatically switches the lights on. Ensure that your lighting units have self-starting ballasts.

During the first few weeks, aerobic bacteria colonize the filter sponge. These will help to break down the waste products from the fish.

Check the thermometer twice a day and keep a note of the reading. Expect it to fluctuate by a degree or so from day to night and even day to day, especially in hot weather.

Adding the fish

Introducing the first fish is one of the most exciting aspects of setting up a new tank. Choose your fish with care, because they will be with you for a few years. The aquarium dealer will pack your fishes in a plastic bag containing a small amount of water and a great deal of air. This should then be put into a paper bag, as fish kept in the dark during transportation suffer less stress. This in turn is often placed into a carrier bag.

If the weather is very hot or cold, it is a wise precaution to take along an insulated box or bag to ensure that the fish do not overheat or chill on the journey home. Go straight home after buying your fish so that they spend the least possible time in transit and therefore are subject to less stress. The aim is to give them the best possible start.

2 If the fish have had a longer trip home, it is always worth opening the bag to provide some fresh air for the them. Carefully roll down the sides of the bag and hook it over the edge of the aquarium to stop it being moved around by the flow of water. You can leave it like this to equalize water temperature.

1 When you arrive home, carefully remove the outer carrier bag and the inner paper bag.

A common fallacy

It has long been held that mixing small amounts of tank water with that in the bag will enable the fish to become accustomed to small changes in water chemistry. This is a pointless exercise as it takes a fish days, not minutes or hours, to adjust to such changes.

3 When the temperatures have equalized, release the fish gently into the tank. Do not just tip the bag upside down! Turn it gently onto its side and hold the top open with one hand while slowly upending the bottom to encourage the fish to swim out.

The furnished tank with your first fish

Having released your fish, quietly and carefully replace the condensation tray and hood. Switch on the light, sit back, and admire your handiwork.

At first, the fish will take cover in the plants, but it will only be a matter of minutes before they come out to investigate their new home.

When closing the hood, do not let it bang shut as this will frighten the fish.

At first the fish will show poor color; this is quite normal, as they are unsure of their new surroundings. As they gain confidence, their colors will improve.

Keep a check on the temperature, but do not get paranoid about it. Remember a fluctuation of one or two degrees is acceptable.

Options and continuing care

In this part of the book, we start by examining some alternative filtration options. Filtration systems are many and various, cheap and expensive. We chose a simple and effective internal power filter for our aquarium, but you may wish to consider others. If you are setting up a large aquarium, you might choose an external power filter that will be able to provide an increased water flow and give you filtration options.

We also look in a bit more detail at tank decorations and aquarium plants. This will give you some further choices if you cannot find the plant species we have featured in our aquarium setup.

Unexpected events can always occur in an aquarium – some happy, some not. Fish breed, so what do you do if you suddenly find a brood of guppies in the tank? A short section on breeding will provide you with the solution. Similarly, what is the answer to a fish that has become covered in small white spots? Look up the health section for guidance.

Above all, we take a look at maintaining the aquarium that you have so carefully set up. It is impossible to stress too highly the importance of carrying out thorough, regular maintenance. Remembering to replenish stocks of used items, such as filter floss, or to keep spares may seem pedantic, but if a heater fails suddenly, you may not be able to buy a new one immediately.

Setting up a tropical freshwater aquarium is a challenge, but the effort is worthwhile when it culminates in a happy, healthy system. Fishkeeping is a sociable hobby and chatting to people about their fish is half the fun, so enjoy it.

Using an external power filter

Several companies manufacture external power filters. These units vary in size and design, and you need to choose one that is suitable for your particular aquarium. In theory, the unit should turn over the water in the aquarium twice an hour. In practice, it is usually slightly less than this, as the debris collecting in the canister reduces the water flow. The flow rate is normally given on the filter box, in either liters or gallons per hour.

Some units have the inlet and outlet at the top, others have the inlet at the base of the canister and the outlet at the top. The principle is the same for both. Water flows from the aquarium, is drawn through the filter medium and then pumped back into the tank. The main advantages of this system are that it does not take up valuable space in the aquarium, is easy to service, and is both efficient and versatile. The disadvantage is cost; external power filters are more expensive than other forms of filtration, but what price the lives of your fishes?

External power filters are much larger than internal filters and therefore can accommodate more media for beneficial bacteria to colonize. Being sited outside the aquarium, they are also easier to service. Most are supplied with shut-off taps. When these are closed, you can uncouple the filter unit and take it to the sink for cleaning. When cleaning, remember to rinse the filter media (the foam pad and porous pellets) with aquarium water removed during a water change to avoid killing off the bacteria. You can throw away the grubbiest bits of filter floss and replace them with fresh pieces.

Anatomy of an external filter

Pump motor housing incorporating inlet and outlet tubes.

Filter floss to prevent any fine particles being trapped in the impeller.

Activated carbon to remove toxic substances.

Filter floss to stop carbon mixing with the porous pellets.

Porous pellets provide an ideal medium for beneficial bacteria to multiply.

Foam pad to trap large pieces of debris.

The plastic barrel is attached with clips to the pump housing to complete the unit.

Above: This is a typical external power filter. You can vary the media; for example, if you are keeping softwater fish that require acidic conditions, add a small amount of peat contained in a net bag. For hard water, add limestone chips.

Position the intake basket just above the substrate (it looks higher here because there is no substrate). This way, if the worst happens and a pipe comes loose, all the water will not siphon from the tank. A small amount will be left for the fish to survive in.

Position the return so that it is at slightly above or very slightly below the water surface. Here it is shown lower down for photographic purposes; otherwise it would be hidden behind the black trim on the front of the aquarium.

Above: You can use suckers to attach the rigid plastic part of the return pipe to the outer surface of the glass so that it reaches over the glass bars around the top of the tank.

Hang-on external power filters

An alternative approach is to use an outside power filter that hangs on the back of the tank. Water is drawn up into the unit by an impeller and cascades back into the tank over a plastic chute. Such filters carry out mechanical, chemical, and biological filtration and are easy to hide from view in an aquarium housed in a display cabinet.

Alternative decor

In addition to the wood and rocks we examined on pages 20-23, there are other decorative materials available for the aquarium. These include bamboo, in various widths, and pieces of bark, which can be joined together to create the effect of a larger, but fragmented, whole. It is always worth looking out for oddly shaped pieces of bogwood to make a focal point. As well as plain backgrounds, there are "pictorial" styles and plastic structured preformed backgrounds with a natural-looking texture. These are used inside the aquarium, fixed to the rear panel with silicone sealant.

Right: Bamboo canes evoke an Asian stream aquascape. Varnish thin pieces or replace them as they rot away.

This plastic background has a textured surface and is easy to cut to size. Some are designed to represent a rockface or large tree root.

Sunken cities complement similar ornaments used as tank decor.

Left: Large-bore bamboo can be varnished inside and out, but if you are unsure about using the correct resin, leave them untreated and they will last fairly well.

Trees and logs make a useful background for a larger aquarium.

Since bamboo and cork bark will float, they must be weighted down or fixed into position. Wood can be secured by siliconing it to a heavy object, such as a large rock, or onto a flat piece of slate or glass. Place this beneath the substrate, so that the wood is "resting" on the substrate.

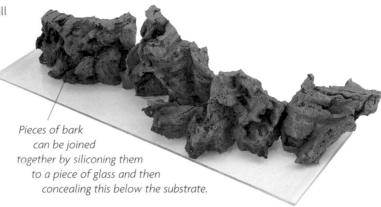

Pieces of bark can be joined together by siliconing them to a piece of glass and then concealing this below the substrate.

Rockwork adds depth to a tank predominantly decorated with rocks of a similar color and texture.

Plant scenes blend in well with planted tanks

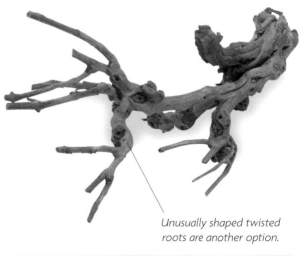

Unusually shaped twisted roots are another option.

Artificial decor

If you prefer not to add rocks and wood to the aquarium, there are some artificial alternatives. Rocklike structures are available in various shapes and sizes that you can use to create instant rock walls, arches, etc. Artificial wood can look very realistic, especially when it is combined with real plants. The advantages of these types of tank decor are that they do not need any preparation (other than a quick wash to remove any dust), and they will not affect the water quality. On the other hand, they are not as individual as natural rocks and wood, and you might find that your friend down the road has exactly the same tank decor as you. If you do use artificial decor, buy all the pieces of, say, wood from the same manufacturer, as each one seems to have their own color scheme and surface texture. Mixing different products can look very unnatural.

Fishkeepers of the future
Tanks containing novelty items attract young children like a magnet. This fascination may be the first sign of an interest in the intriguing world of fishkeeping and, if they offer a route for a prospective aquarist to become involved in the hobby, they are worth considering for inclusion.

These branchlike arrangements are excellent for creating a tangled effect. They also add height to the tank decoration.

Pieces that resemble fallen logs can be used vertically, provided you seat them firmly to prevent them falling over.

You can combine these rocklike structures to create hiding places for fish or position them as individual features in the aquarium.

Artificial wood can look quite realistic, especially if the straight edges are concealed in the substrate.

Of course, a market has developed for novelties in the aquarium, and whether or not you include these is purely a matter of personal choice. If they are sold by one of the major manufacturers, you can be sure that they do not incorporate any toxic substances. Avoid buying cheap plastic novelties of dubious origin, as these may have been manufactured from substances that could harm your fish. Whether your whim is for sunken galleons and divers, underwater cities, or cartoon fish, you will find something suitable. Some items, such as the diver shown here, are air powered. Simply attach an air line to the model and connect it to an air pump. The stream of bubbles rising to the surface not only lends a realistic appearance to the diver, but also helps to agitate the water surface, thus improving the exchange of gases to and from the aquarium.

Make sure your pump can power another item before you buy an air-operated model such as this diver.

Left: *Carefully positioned to allow the free passage of water and access to equipment, artificial rock structures are useful for concealing uplift tubes, heaters, etc.*

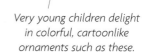

Very young children delight in colorful, cartoonlike ornaments such as these.

Background plants

The plants along the back of the aquarium should all be tall-growing species, and groups often look better than individual plants. In the larger aquarium, big-leaved plants, such as the larger *Echinodorus* species, can be used either singly or in well-spaced groups. As they can look quite imposing and often do not mix well with smaller-leaved stem plants, try complementing them with large pieces of rock or wood. On the other hand, bushy stem plants, such as *Cabomba, Limnophila,* or *Myriophyllum* species, work well when grouped together and combine with adjacent, tall but small-leaved stem plants, such as *Rotala, Egeria, Bacopa,* or *Ludwigia* species.

Left: Limnophila aquatica *will grow well under fluorescent lights, and its lacy texture of fine leaves will add an attractive backdrop to midground and foreground aquarium plants.*

Hygrophila polysperma

Right: *Milfoil* (Myriophyllum aquaticum) *will do well in most tanks, particularly if you regularly add a multipurpose fertilizer to the water and provide bright metal-halide lighting.*

Background planting

Suitable background plants include Bacopa caroliniana • Cabomba caroliniana • Crinum thaianum • Echinodorus species • Egeria densa • Hygrophila polysperma • Limnophila aquatica • Ludwigia palustris • Myriophyllum aquaticum • Rotala macrandra • Vallisneria americana

Positioning plants

In areas of water flow, such as those near the filter outlet, the best background plants are those with long, narrow leaves. They are suited to the constant disturbance and create an element of movement in the aquarium. *Vallisneria* and *Crinum* species are ideal. Background planting can be extended around the sides of the aquarium to create a more enclosed environment and a "border" for the display.

Plants can be grouped and placed in a number of different ways to create an interesting design. Although it is tempting to use many different species, it is often easier and more effective to use a limited number of species in larger groupings.

Straight vallis is tall, with fairly brittle leaves that snap easily. You may be misled by its scientific name, Vallisneria spiralis. *The "spiralis" refers to the flower stems that spiral upward.*

Above: *Twisted vallis gets its name from its attractive twisted leaves. It tends not to grow as tall as straight vallis. Propagate by runners.*

Leaf shapes vary in species of Amazon swordplants. Use those with large, leaves to create shady areas in the aquarium.

*The broadleaved Amazon swordplant (*Echinodorus paniculatus*) tolerates a range of water conditions, including hard alkaline water.*

51

Midground plants

The midground is simply a "mixing" of the foreground and background. Plants that can be trimmed to variable heights are ideal here. Creating a "street" grouping of one particular plant, with taller specimens in the background, and others gradually becoming shorter towards the foreground blends areas together. *Alternanthera, Bacopa, Heteranthera, Hygrophila,* and *Lysimachia* species are excellent for this purpose.

Bacopa caroliniana *is a good plant for the mid-zone of the tank. Remove the lowest pair of leaves before planting and take care, as the stems bruise easily.*

Taking cuttings of aquarium plants

Some cuttings of popular aquarium plants are collected from the wild during the dry season in the tropical regions in which they grow. During this time, the plants have woody stems and may flower, and the leaf shapes differ from the submersed form. It is easy to tell if the plants have been growing out of water, or emersed; hold the base of the stem and the plant will remain upright. If you try this with a plant grown underwater, it will flop over because the water normally holds it up. You can use these woody cuttings to create underwater plants for your aquarium. Plant them in a spare tank full of water and wait. Remove the leaves as they die off and, after a short time, shoots appear from some leaf joints. Cut off these underwater growths and plant them as normal cuttings. What you have done is to repeat the normal cycle of the plant in the wild and provided it with a sudden rainy season. It has responded by producing its underwater leaves that enable it to survive. These are often softer and of a different shape and color to its emersed leaves.

Many aquarium plants are now mist-propagated to prevent undue pressures on wild stocks. They may shed a few leaves when submerged, but this is quite natural, and they will soon recover.

Midground planting

Midground plants include: Alternanthera reineckii Anubias barteri Bacopa monnieri Cardamine lyrata Didiplis diandra Heteranthera zosterifolia Hydrocotyle species Lysimachia nummularia Microsorium pteropus

Sagittaria platyphylla *is a versatile plant that can be used singly in open spaces, as a middle-ground plant, or grouped toward the center of the aquarium. Provide bright lighting and a good supply of iron.*

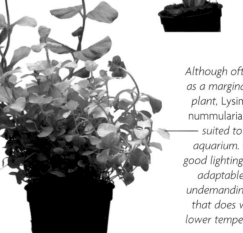

Although often sold as a marginal pond plant, Lysimachia nummularia *is also suited to the aquarium. Given good lighting, it is an adaptable and undemanding plant that does well at lower temperatures.*

Above: *The unusual branching appearance of the leaves and stems of* Hydrocotyle leucocephala *make it a distinctive plant for the midground.*

Foreground plants • Floating plants

The foreground of the aquarium provides an open swimming area and should not become an "underwater jungle," but depending on the size of the tank, one or two "carpet-forming" plant species can cover an open substrate without intruding on the swimming space. It is also a good site for individual specimen plants, such as *Anubias barteri* growing on a piece of bogwood, either in their own space or among the carpet-forming species.

Right: *Here, Monosolenium tenerum is growing on a clay "stone" that can be placed where it is to grow in the foreground.*

Cryptocoryne willisii is a tiny species growing to no more than 1.6-2 in (4-5 cm). In good light it will spread across an open area.

Small-leaved Micranthemum umbrosum is easy to grow. Trim growth to keep it in shape.

Above: Eleocharis acicularis, *has grasslike foliage that is appreciated by small fish.*

Foreground planting

Anubias barteri var. nana
Cryptocoryne willisii
Echinodorus tenellus
Eleocharis parvula
Lilaeopsis novae-zelandiae
Marsilea hirsuta
Micranthemum umbrosum
Monosolenium tenerum
Sagittaria pusilla
Samolus valerandi
Vesicularia dubyana

Floating plants perform several useful roles in the aquarium. Primarily, they add a touch of "real life" to the display, echoing the plant-strewn surface waters of rivers and lakes in the wild. They also provide welcome shade for other plants and cover for surface-dwelling fishes. Floating plants establish quickly in the aquarium and will flourish in a well lit environment.

Floating plants

Ceratophyllum spp.
Ceratopteris spp.
Eichhornia crassipes
Limnobium laevigatum
Ludwigia helminthorrhiza
Pistia stratiotes
Riccia fluitans
Salvinia natans

Below: *Although hornwort (Ceratophyllum demersum) is often planted in the substrate, it is really a floating species and suited to cool conditions.*

Left: *The fleshy leaves of* Pistia stratiotes *have a covering of tiny hairs, giving them a velvety texture. Provide good ventilation and bright metal-halide lighting.*

Right: *The finely feathered roots of Salvinia natans are able to take up the maximum amount of nutrients from the water and make hiding places for fish.*

Attaching a plant to wood

Some plants, such as this Java fern, prefer to be planted on objects such as wood and porous rocks, rather than in the substrate. This is most useful when you are trying to create height in an aquarium or if you are keeping fish that dig in the substrate.

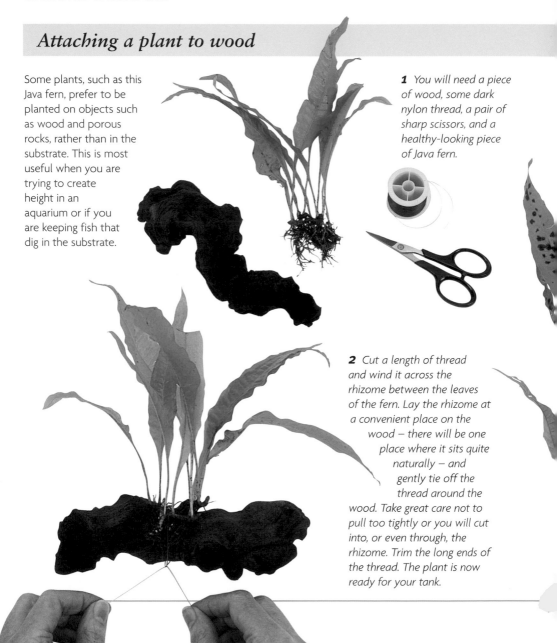

1 *You will need a piece of wood, some dark nylon thread, a pair of sharp scissors, and a healthy-looking piece of Java fern.*

2 *Cut a length of thread and wind it across the rhizome between the leaves of the fern. Lay the rhizome at a convenient place on the wood – there will be one place where it sits quite naturally – and gently tie off the thread around the wood. Take great care not to pull too tightly or you will cut into, or even through, the rhizome. Trim the long ends of the thread. The plant is now ready for your tank.*

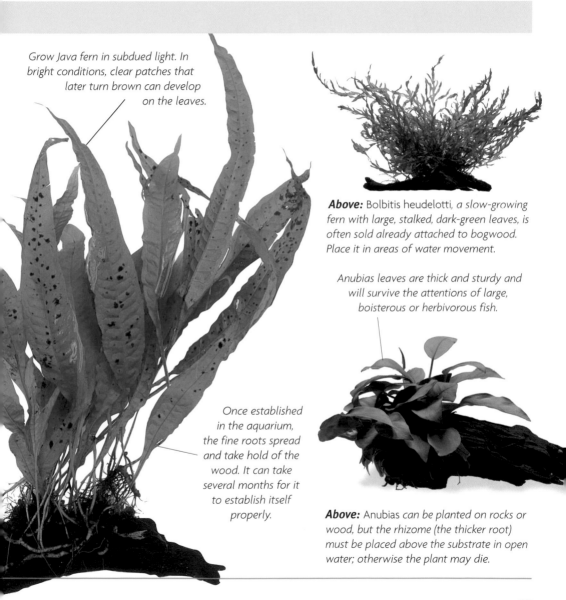

Grow Java fern in subdued light. In bright conditions, clear patches that later turn brown can develop on the leaves.

Above: Bolbitis heudelotti, *a slow-growing fern with large, stalked, dark-green leaves, is often sold already attached to bogwood. Place it in areas of water movement.*

Anubias leaves are thick and sturdy and will survive the attentions of large, boisterous or herbivorous fish.

Once established in the aquarium, the fine roots spread and take hold of the wood. It can take several months for it to establish itself properly.

Above: Anubias *can be planted on rocks or wood, but the rhizome (the thicker root) must be placed above the substrate in open water; otherwise the plant may die.*

Using plastic plants in the aquarium

These days, you can choose from a wide range of very realistic plastic plants. They are not to everyone's taste, but they do have their uses, especially if you have fish that are continually uprooting plants. They are easy to position; just sink the tray at the base of the plant into the gravel to hold it in place. You can also pull plastic plants apart and slot them back together again to lengthen or shorten them. Best of all, if they get covered in algae you can take them out and scrub them clean. On the other hand, plastic plants are inert so they will do nothing to assist in the removal of nitrates from the tank as real plants would. It is essential, therefore, that you pay very particular attention to regular water changes and the efficiency of your filtration system. Plastic plants are probably best used in conjunction with a few real ones.

Cabomba
Elegant fine foliage, but may be difficult to keep clean.

Vallisneria
Straplike leaves that contrast well with other plants.

Moneywort
The broad leaves are good for hiding pipes and heaters.

Below: To achieve a thicket of plants, choose two or three of the same type, but vary the heights. This is easy to do; just split the stems and add or remove sections until you have a stem of the desired length.

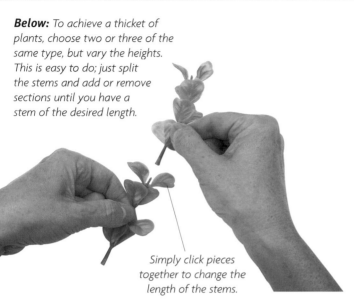

Simply click pieces together to change the length of the stems.

Above: Plastic plants are easy to position in the aquarium. Simply hold the plant at the base and push it firmly into the substrate so that it cannot be seen.

Elodea
Use different lengths to create thickets in the aquarium.

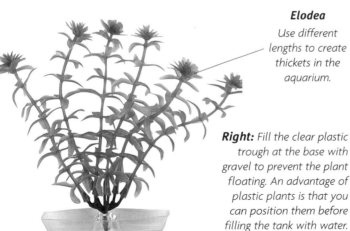

Right: Fill the clear plastic trough at the base with gravel to prevent the plant floating. An advantage of plastic plants is that you can position them before filling the tank with water.

59

Foods and feeding

Just like any living thing, fish need food to survive, and the only way they can get it is when you give it to them. In the wild they can swim up- or downstream to where their preferred food is abundant, but in the confines of the aquarium, they have only what they are given. Always consider the fish's natural diet and offer it the equivalent commercial food. A vast range of foods has been developed to cater for all manner of fish needs and the array of pots and packets can be confusing, so it is best that we look at each type of food in turn.

Above: *To avoid polluting the water, offer fish only as much flake food as they will consume in 10-15 minutes.*

Tablet foods

These are much like flake foods, but in another form. Some "stick" on the side of the tank and are ideal for midwater community fish. Sinking tablets benefit some of the bottom-dwelling fish.

Freeze-dried foods

These are available as small cubes, here tubifex.

Freeze-dried foods

These are also sold as fine, loose food, here mosquito larvae.

Sinking granules

These are suitable for bottom-dwelling catfishes.

Storing foods

Dried foods will lose nutritional value once the container is open. Buy small quantities – enough for 30-45 days. Store any large opened containers in a freezer.

Right: *The shape, size and position of the mouth is a good indicator of how a fish feeds and what size food it can consume.*

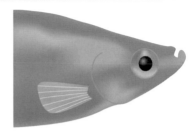

Left: *As it disintegrates, a food tablet "stuck" to the glass attracts fish from all over the tank.*

A longer lower jaw shows how the fish feeds by approaching food from beneath.

Floating food sticks

These are useful for feeding the larger barbs.

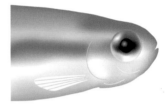

Terminal mouths are typical of midwater fish and allow the fish to approach their food head-on.

Dried foods

These are available in various forms and can provide the staple diet for most fish. Offer them sparingly, as left uneaten, they can quickly pollute the aquarium. Flake foods are the most common form. They have been developed to accommodate the needs of herbivores and carnivores, and also to enhance the color of fish.

Extended upper jaws are seen on fish that approach food from above, such as bottom dwellers.

Foods and feeding

Feeding your fish once a day is fine. A hungry (but not starving) fish is a healthy fish. With dried and frozen foods, feed only what the fish will consume in about 10-15 minutes. The rules are different for herbivores; you can leave the green food in the tank until the next feed, but remove the old food before offering fresh supplies. Start with small amounts, such as a small pinch of flake, one or two tablets, or a single lettuce leaf, and increase or decrease the amount as necessary.

When you feed the fish will depend on the fish you are keeping. Some like to come out at dawn and dusk, while others will feed during the day. Fortunately for us, fish obligingly change some of their feeding habits in the confines of the aquarium, and will come out as soon as they sense food. Just be sure to check that the food is reaching all the fish.

Fish benefit greatly from variety in their diet. Use a dried food as a basis, but offer some frozen or live foods once or twice a week. Live and frozen foods help to maintain the sheen on the body of your fish and are good for growing young fish into healthy adults.

Left: Pop the frozen pea between your finger and thumb to release the inner seed. Discard the seed coats because fish tend to get trapped in them.

Below: There are a number of green foods that you can feed to herbivorous fish. Offer them regularly and the fish will leave your plants alone. Remove any uneaten leaves. An overnight stay in the freezer will soften kale and broad-leaved parsley.

Lettuce leaves
"Plant" these in the substrate for the fish to graze on. Left to float, the fish usually ignore them.

Frozen peas
These are taken by many fish, other than the strict herbivores.

Courgette and potato
Parboil slices until the surface is soft but will not break up. These items may also be fed uncooked.

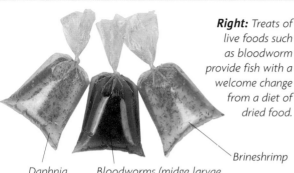

Right: *Treats of live foods such as bloodworm provide fish with a welcome change from a diet of dried food.*

Brineshrimp

Daphnia
(water fleas)

Bloodworms (midge larvae
of a blood-red color)

Above: *Aquatic live foods include mosquito larvae and pupae, daphnia, and bloodworms. These can be safely collected from a pond, providing it does not contain fish. Live tubifex are best avoided, as they inhabit polluted mud, but the freeze-dried alternative is safe.*

Fresh frozen irradiated foods

These are sold as individual portions in foil-sealed trays. Simply pop one out and drop it into the tank, where it quickly defrosts.

When defrosted, one cube of frozen bloodworms provides a good "meaty" meal for larger or spawning fishes.

Holiday feeding

If you plan to be away for more than a week or two, package up daily rations of flake or freeze-dried food in a twist of foil and leave them for a friend to administer. Alternatively, invest in an autofeeder – a timer-controlled reservoir for flake or small granules – and program it to dispense one or more meals daily. The battery-operated feeder shown here is easy to program. At the preset times, the food compartment rotates and the contents drop into the tank. Adjust the blue wheel to control the feed quantity.

Breeding your fish

Although you may not set out with any intention of breeding your fish, there is every chance that if conditions are to their liking, they will breed. If this happens, the question is what do you do next?

The tropical species you are keeping fall into two groups: livebearers and egglayers. The first young fish you are likely to encounter in the community aquarium are the young of livebearing fishes.

Livebearers

As their name suggests, these fish give birth to fully formed live young. They are usually quite large and the brood is a manageable size. Being larger than the fry that hatch from eggs, they have a reasonable chance of survival in the community tank, but some will fall prey to the other fish. They are able to nibble at the edge of flaked food and will pick at algae on plants. To help feed them, you can crumble some flake food or add one of the liquid suspension foods manufactured for livebearers.

You also need to consider that these extra bodies, however small at present, will grow and thus increase your stocking levels beyond the capacity of the aquarium and its life support system (the filter). In short, you will need another tank. A tank measuring 18x10x10 in (45x25x25 cm) makes a useful rearing tank. And when it is not being used for this purpose, it makes an ideal emergency quarantine tank. Set up the tank as normal. Partially fill it with

water from the main aquarium and add a small amount of fresh water. (Top up the main tank with fresh water as if you were doing a water change.) In this way, you have combined aged water from the main tank with a little fresh and can safely net and transfer the youngsters to the rearing tank without having to wait for the water to age; in effect you have done a water change on both tanks. Take care with the level of feeding; keep it low until the filter has had a chance to build up enough bacteria to cope. The amount of time fry spend in rearing tanks depends on their growth rate. Do not put them with other fish until they are large enough not to be eaten. If you have too many fry, give them to friends or take them to your local aquarium club or shop.

Above: Female platies often give birth in the aquarium. They seek out a quiet place, frequently near the water surface in the shelter of plants, and this gives the fry a chance to escape predation.

Breeding setup

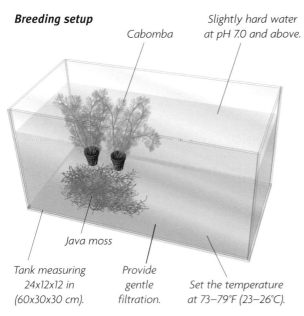

Cabomba

Slightly hard water at pH 7.0 and above.

Java moss

Tank measuring 24x12x12 in (60x30x30 cm).

Provide gentle filtration.

Set the temperature at 73–79°F (23–26°C).

Female

Male

Floating plants, such as Salvinia auriculata, *provide shelter and spawning sites for surface-spawning fish.*

Above: *In the platies* (Xiphophorus maculatus) *the sexes are easily told apart by the anal fin. In the male it has become modified into an internal organ of fertilization known as a gonopodium.*

Left: *Liquid fry foods for livebearers and egglayers contain the food in suspension.*

65

Breeding your fish

Egglayers are a little more difficult to cope with. Although some species will spawn in the community aquarium, only species that actively protect their eggs and fry, such as cichlids, succeed in raising a brood. It is far better to set up a breeding tank with whatever the fish require (fine-leaved plants, spawning mops, caves, slate, etc.) and spawn the fish in this. Depending on species – and you will need to find out about the fish you are intending to spawn – you should remove one or both parents after spawning and return them to the main aquarium or leave them to tend the eggs and subsequent fry.

Conditioning the parents is important. Again, investigate the species you are keeping and feed them on the correct foods to bring them into spawning condition before you try to breed them.

Feeding the fry of egglayers is full of problems. Sometimes the fry are so tiny that they will eat only infusoria, tiny microscopic creatures that you have to culture. Others are slightly larger and need newly hatched brine shrimp. For these you can buy brine shrimp eggs to hatch in saline water. Fortunately, some fry – but by no means all – will take some of the fine commercial livebearer fry foods available in either liquid or powder form. Other fry will require green foods in the form of algae, frozen peas, and lettuce leaves.

Making a spawning mop

1 Wind nylon wool around a piece of card or the short side of this book until you have about 30 strands. Cut off the surplus. Green is the preferred color because it looks more natural.

2 Cut another piece of wool about 8 in (20 cm) long from the ball and thread it under the strands. Secure the strands with a tight knot.

3 Turn over the card or book and cut the strands at a point opposite the knot. You now have a spawning mop. Wash it under the tap in warm (not boiling) water before using it.

4 The long ends of wool securing the mop strands can be used to tie the mop to a cork or to suspend it from the surface of the aquarium.

Raising fry successfully

Whichever kind of fish you are breeding, cleanliness is all-important. Eggs can quickly become fungused if conditions are poor in the aquarium or the eggs are infertile, and tiny fry can contract bacterial infections in dirty conditions.

Another cause of losses is starvation, either because you do not have food ready when the fry need it or because you are feeding foods that are simply too large for the fry to eat. It does not matter how much food you regularly put into the tank; if it is the wrong size or offered at the wrong time, the fish will starve. More fish are probably lost for these reasons than for any other.

Right: By first attaching the spawning mops to corks, you can suspend them at intervals along the water surface.

Above: Eggs can just be seen developing in the deep body of a marbled hatchetfish (Carnegiella strigata). This top-swimming fish is mirrored in the surface of the water.

Left: To establish a supply of infusoria to feed young fry, place a piece of lightly boiled potato in a jar of old aquarium water and leave it open to the air.

Right: After about a week in a warm, light spot, the water will be cloudy with infusoria. Simply pour some into the tank.

Health care

It is difficult to admit, but most of the problems that happen in a fish tank are down to us. The major reason for things going wrong is poor water quality because we forget or delay doing something about it. This is when you begin to see the benefit of keeping an aquarium log. Get yourself a notebook, and each time you do something to your tank, write down the date and what you did, because it is very easy to forget! Did you do the water change last week or was it the week before? Also note down observations such as behavior patterns, as any change may alert you to a potential problem or event. The log helps to get you into the habit of looking, seeing what your looking at, and acting on it.

Keeping the water in good condition is the key to successful fishkeeping. It means that you must carry out regular water changes and ensure that your filtration system is working properly. Your fish will indicate that there may be a potential problem. If they hang near the surface, the chances are that oxygen levels are low. Check the temperature and the flow from your filter, and correct as necessary. Remember that during hot summer months the temperature can rise above normal levels even when the thermostat has switched your heater off. At such times, a water change and increasing the water flow from your filter or adding an airstone

Right: Catfishes rely on their sensitive barbels to locate and taste food items in the substrate. Provide a smooth substrate and good water conditions to prevent damage to the barbels.

to increase turbulence at the water surface will help.

Another common problem is stress caused by incompatible tankmates or poor conditions. This can weaken a fish so that it becomes an easy target for illness. Choose your fish with care.

Buying healthy fish

Fish travel long distances to get to our tanks. They may have been bred on farms in the Far East, then caught and transported to packing stations, where

Left: Always start by buying healthy stock, such as this tiger barb. Once the retailer has netted your chosen fish into a plastic bag, hold it up and examine it carefully. There should be no sign of split fins, deformities, or ulcers.

they are repacked for air shipment to us. On arrival, they are driven to a wholesaler, who unpacks them and rests them before they go on sale to retailers. Again they are packed and transported to the retail outlet, where they are finally unpacked, rested, and put on sale. What happens when we buy them? They are packed, yet again, and taken home by us. All this can be stressful and, despite all the best endeavors at each stage of the process, some fish will fall ill and some will perish.

Do not be surprised if you see tanks in quarantine at your local shop or notices that say something like "New arrivals, not on sale yet." This is your retailer looking after his stock and a sign of a good shop.

When you buy your fish, check to see that they are active and behaving normally. For example, shoaling fish should be swimming about with their fins held out, whereas bottom-dwelling species will be grubbing about on the substrate searching for food. Avoid fish with split fins or badly damaged barbels, as both can be sites of potential secondary fungal or bacterial infection. Avoid fish with pinched-looking bellies or sunken eyes; they may not be feeding properly or may have internal parasites.

Quarantine strategy

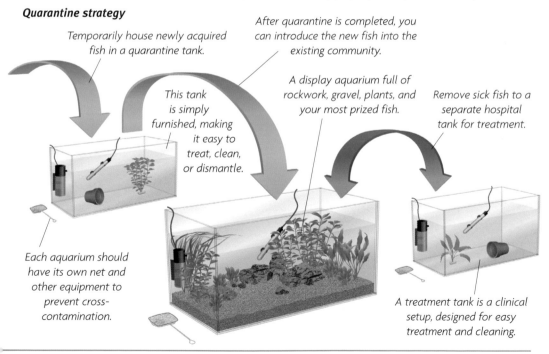

Temporarily house newly acquired fish in a quarantine tank.

After quarantine is completed, you can introduce the new fish into the existing community.

This tank is simply furnished, making it easy to treat, clean, or dismantle.

A display aquarium full of rockwork, gravel, plants, and your most prized fish.

Remove sick fish to a separate hospital tank for treatment.

Each aquarium should have its own net and other equipment to prevent cross-contamination.

A treatment tank is a clinical setup, designed for easy treatment and cleaning.

Health care

The problems described on these pages are by no means the only ones that can occur in an aquarium, but they are the main ones that you are likely to encounter. All are easily treated, provided they are caught early – a key factor in keeping your aquarium healthy. Some will respond to a simple water change, others will need medication. Before you buy any medication, make sure you have diagnosed the problem correctly – do not guess; dosing with the wrong product will not cure the problem. And give the medication time to work. It is not instant; indeed, some take several days. Certain medications can be unsuitable for some fish species, so read the label carefully before buying a product and, if in doubt, ask. The efficacy of medications deteriorates with time, so it is best to buy them as you need them. Never overdose; follow all the instructions, or the result can be fatal. And above all, never mix medications; a lethal concoction can result.

White spot

Caused by a parasite, *Ichthyophthirius multifiliis*, these small creatures are noticeable at the stage when they appear as small white spots on the body and fins of their host. They spend time under the skin of the fish until they mature, when they break out and fall to the bottom of the aquarium and form cysts. Within each cyst, cell division produces over 1000 new parasites. When the cyst ruptures, they break out to infect a new host. It is during this free-swimming stage that white spot can be effectively treated. Treat the whole tank using a proprietary white spot cure and follow the instructions carefully.

Fungus

Fungus is a secondary infection that gets into wounds when the body mucus has been damaged by injury, environmental factors, or parasites. (One fish picking at another's fins is a prime cause.) It manifests itself as fluffy cotton wool-like growths on the body and/or fins. For minor outbreaks, spot treat the site of infection with a proprietary aquarium fungicide. For major outbreaks, treat the whole tank. Above all, remedy the cause.

Left: *A typical outbreak of white spot, as seen on this harlequin rasbora, will respond to prompt treatment of the whole tank with a proprietary aquarium remedy.*

Fin rot

This problem is typical of poorly maintained tanks. It shows itself as a degeneration of the fin membranes, so that the fin rays stick out and the fins may look sore and inflamed. If caught early, a simple water change and overhaul of the filter system to restore its efficiency will rectify the problem. In more advanced cases, spot treat or treat the whole tank with an aquarium bactericide, depending on how many fish are affected.

Spotting fin rot

The fins of a fish are normally smooth around the edge, although some may be naturally scalloped.

In poor conditions, the membrane between the fin rays degenerates, leaving the rays sticking out unevenly.

Degeneration and erosion of barbels

There are two causes for this condition: poor water conditions and using a sharp substrate. If your fish have barbels and you have an outbreak of fin rot, the chances are that the barbels will degenerate to the point where parts of them break off. Remedy as for fin rot, as described above. If the cause is erosion, the only solution is to change the substrate. The delicate barbels on catfish and loaches can be cut by sharp grains of gravel or sand and secondary fungal and bacterial infections can then set in.

Split fins

If there is a lot of bickering going on in the tank, split, torn, or completely ragged fins are a likely outcome. Watch to see which fish is the culprit and remove it. If the victim is fit and well, the fins normally heal themselves, but look for any signs of secondary infections from fungus or bacteria and treat as necessary.

Disposing of sick fish humanely

Fill a bowl with a quart of water from the aquarium and mix in a minimum of 10 drops of clove oil before putting in the affected fish.

Adding medication to the aquarium

Left: Calculate the correct amount of medication, following the directions exactly. Fill a container with aquarium water and add the medication to it.

Left: Thoroughly mix the medication into the water and pour it into the tank. Diluting it first reduces the risk of producing localized spots of dangerously high concentrations.

Routine maintenance

To keep your fish and plants healthy in the closed system of an aquarium, you need to carry out regular maintenance – an hour or so once a week will usually suffice. You will need to carry out some maintenance tasks every day, others every two weeks, some monthly, and others less frequently. These timescales are only a guide, since each tank will vary, depending on its size, the method of filtration, and the number of fish you keep.

By noting all your actions in an aquarium log you will soon see a pattern developing that is right for your aquarium. Should something occur at the wrong time, you can refer back to see what has changed and you might have the answer to your problem.

Checking the temperature and health of your fish will become automatic when you pass the tank. Brush your hand against the glass and get used to the "feel" of the tank at the correct temperature. Observe how your fish behave and you will learn to notice slight alterations that are indications that there may be a problem on the way.

Water changes

The first major maintenance task will be a water change, and the purpose of this is to reduce the nitrates that can

build up in the tank. (See page 26.) For this you need a bucket (it is best to keep one specifically for aquarium use), a length of clear plastic siphon tubing, and a siphon starter so that you do not get a mouthful of tank water when sucking on the tube to start it. Place the bucket on the floor, place one end of the tube in the tank and start your siphon. Watch

The tap pump connects to most tap fittings and can either create suction to clean the tank or allow water to pass through to fill the tank.

Push the tube into the gravel. Dirt and gravel swirl inside the tube and the lighter debris is drawn off by siphon action.

A flow adjuster controls the speed of filling and/or cleaning. Keep it free of debris.

A flexible hose (shortened here) takes water to and from the aquarium.

Safety first
Before you start any routine maintenance work on your aquarium, unplug all the electrical appliances such as filters and heaters.

that you do not suck up any fish and also try to avoid spraying the water over your feet! When you get used to it, you will be able to suck up all the mulm (organic debris) on the substrate as you do your water change, thus doing two jobs at once. Take out 10-20% of the water. Before you throw the water away just check to make sure there are no life forms in it – you would not be the first person to throw a fish out with the tank water!

While the water level is down, tidy up the plants by removing any dead or badly damaged leaves. You can also clean the front glass with an algae magnet or scraper to remove any algal growth.

Top up the tank with conditioned water at the right temperature, either by siphoning it into the tank or by gently pouring it in with a jug. Before replacing the condensation tray or cover glass check that it is clean so that it does not cut down the amount of light available to the plants.

Testing the nitrite level

Keeping a check on the nitrite levels in the tank is a worthwhile exercise. Test kits are quite easy to use. Always use a clean, dry vial so that the sample is not contaminated. Nitrite levels will fluctuate slightly and will certainly vary before and after a water change. After the initial peak during maturation, they should be negligible, but may rise when you have cleaned your filter, because you have flushed away some of the beneficial bacteria and these will take a little time to build up again. Reducing feeding at this time to ease the load on the filter will help.

Above: *Water is sucked up the wide tube of the gravel cleaner by siphonic action and whisks away the debris.*

Above: *Trimming unruly plant stems encourages strong new growth and keeps plants looking tidy.*

Cleaning the internal filter

Cleaning filters is a necessary evil when you keep fish! Filters should smell organic; if they have a foul, putrid odour, they are not working properly. Luckily, this only happens if the air supply or water flow has been disrupted for several hours, preventing oxygen reaching the filter media. After this time, the aerobic bacteria have begun to die and anaerobic bacteria have stated to colonize the media. For this reason, you should never turn off your filter system for any longer than the time it takes to service it. When cleaning a filter, always use water removed from the aquarium during the water change; otherwise you risk killing off the bacteria living in the filter medium. And, for the same reason, never use any detergents.

1 *Carefully remove the internal power filter from its supporting cradle and lift it from the tank without any debris falling back into the aquarium. It is a good idea to have a bowl or bucket ready to put it in, as it saves leaving a trail of drips all the way to the sink.*

2 *Over a bowl or bucket, carefully separate the motor from the canister. You can place the canister in the bowl while you deal with the motor.*

3 Clean any filter pads and impellers that may have become clogged with dirt and wipe off any slime on the plastic. Check the bearings and replace them if necessary.

4 Remove the sponge from the canister and rinse it in water from the aquarium to remove all the fine debris. Take out any other parts, such as screens and dividers, and wipe them clean.

Useful spares

Make sure that you have the following spares available at all times, and remember to replace the ones you use.

Heater-thermostat
Suckers
Diaphragms and
filter pads for
air pumps
Bearings, impeller,
and O-ring seals
for filters
Filter floss and/or
sponges
Other media if used
Activated carbon
Thermometer
Nets

Fuses
Battery-operated
airpump and
batteries
(do not keep them
in the pump but
with it)
Air line
Airstones
Starter for the
lights

5 Once you have finished cleaning all the parts, reassemble the filter and put it back in the tank. Turn on the electricity and make sure the filter is working.

Keeping your aquarium running smoothly

Certain routine tasks need only be carried out once or twice a year. One of these is replacing the fluorescent tubes in the lighting hood. Even if the tubes seem to be working normally, their useful light output will have diminished, and this can affect plant growth. Keep tubes, reflectors, and cover glasses dust-free. Check that the endcaps on the starter unit have not perished or become brittle, that leads have not chafed against the hood, and that plastic securing clips still grip the tubes tightly.

Three ways to clean the tank glass

1 *A wad of filter wool will remove algae and debris from the interior glass surface.*

2 *The rough surface of a scraper on the end of a handle deals with stubborn marks.*

3 *To use a magnetic algae cleaner, place the magnet faced with the scouring material inside the tank and guide it from outside with the other magnet.*

Check equipment such as filters, air pumps, heaters, and lights every day to confirm they are functioning properly.

Clean the front aquarium glass every 7-14 days to remove algae.

Prune bunch plants regularly and replant the cuttings. Remove dead vegetation every 7-14 days.

Check the fish every day.

Remove debris from the substrate every 7-14 days.

Replace the lighting tubes every 6-12 months.

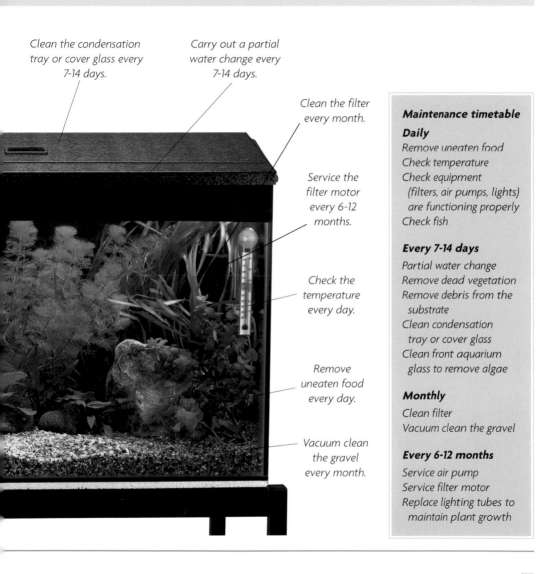

Clean the condensation tray or cover glass every 7-14 days.

Carry out a partial water change every 7-14 days.

Clean the filter every month.

Service the filter motor every 6-12 months.

Check the temperature every day.

Remove uneaten food every day.

Vacuum clean the gravel every month.

Maintenance timetable

Daily
Remove uneaten food
Check temperature
Check equipment
  (filters, air pumps, lights)
  are functioning properly
Check fish

Every 7-14 days
Partial water change
Remove dead vegetation
Remove debris from the
  substrate
Clean condensation
  tray or cover glass
Clean front aquarium
  glass to remove algae

Monthly
Clean filter
Vacuum clean the gravel

Every 6-12 months
Service air pump
Service filter motor
Replace lighting tubes to
  maintain plant growth

PART THREE

Introduction to fish profiles

The whole purpose of setting up your aquarium is to keep fish and, in this case, tropical freshwater fish. You will probably have gazed at the tanks in your local aquarium shop and decided which fishes you would like to keep. This part of the book presents a selection of fishes, with guidance on the conditions they need to thrive in your aquarium.

Although all the fish featured here are tropical, this does not mean that they all require the same water temperatures. Even in the tropics there are variations depending on altitude and type of habitat. Swift-flowing mountain streams are cool and highly oxygenated, whereas the lower courses of rivers can be sluggish and poorly oxygenated. Lakes have differing zones of temperature, while still pools can be very hot, very low in oxygen, and may even evaporate. You need to take all these factors into account when keeping tropical fish and

ensure that you keep them within their favored range of conditions.

Setting up a balanced community of fishes in an aquarium means taking into account the needs of a particular species as well as the compatibility between fish species. It is also vital to know what size of tank suits each fish and what regions they inhabit within the tank. Reading through the main text for each species will provide this information.

The fish are arranged in groups, but bear in mind that within some groups there are several families. The majority of cyprinids, characins, livebearers, and anabantids are midwater-swimming fish that should be kept in shoals, pairs, or trios. The catfishes and loaches are mainly bottom-dwellers. The fish within the four remaining groups — killifishes, rainbowfishes, gobies, and cichlids — have slightly more specific needs and are recommended for fishkeepers with 6-12 months experience.

Understanding your fish

Throughout this part of the book we mention the names of fins and other parts of the body. The illustrations here will help you understand what we are talking about. If you turn back to them every now and then the terms will soon begin to stick in your mind.

The gills, located beneath the gill cover (or operculum), allow the fish to breathe by extracting oxygen from the water.

Typical cyprinid (barbs, danios, rasboras, etc.)

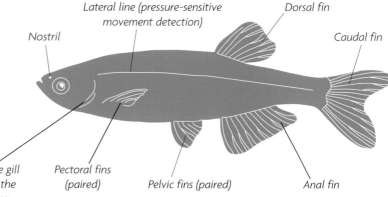

Lateral line (pressure-sensitive movement detection)

Nostril

Dorsal fin

Caudal fin

Pectoral fins (paired)

Pelvic fins (paired)

Anal fin

Typical armored catfish

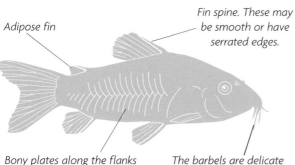

Adipose fin

Fin spine. These may be smooth or have serrated edges.

Bony plates along the flanks protect the body but make it inflexible, so these fish are poor swimmers.

The barbels are delicate sensory organs that can be easily damaged.

Typical male livebearer

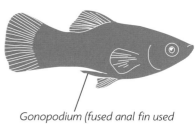

Gonopodium (fused anal fin used for internal fertilization).

Fish measurements

The sizes of fishes given throughout the book refer to the length of the body, excluding the tail fin.

Levels in the aquarium

The top layer of water to a depth of about 2 in (5 cm) is home to fish that swim and feed at the surface, such as the marbled hatchetfish.

The biggest zone in the tank is the middle layer, where you will find shoaling fish, such as neon tetras and other midwater swimmers.

Fish such as catfishes and loaches will feel at home at the bottom of the tank.

Number of tropical fish to a tank

Surface area is the governing factor for the number of fish you can keep in an aquarium. For tropical freshwater species you need 12 sq in (75 sq cm) of surface area per 1 in (2.5 cm) body length (do not include the tail) of fish. A tank measuring 24x12 in (60x30 cm) has a surface area of 288 sq in (1800 sq cm) and will hold about 24 in (60 cm) of freshwater tropical fish. Allow for growth when choosing fish.

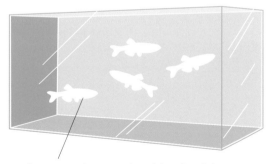

This 24x12 in (60x30 cm) tank has four fish, each measuring 6 in (15 cm) long, which together add up to the maximum carrying capacity of 24 in (60 cm) of fish body length.

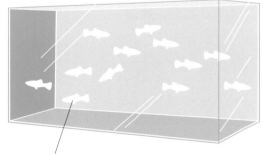

This 24x12 in (60x30 cm) tank has 12 fish, each measuring 2 in (5 cm) long, which together add up to the maximum carrying capacity of 24 in (60 cm) of fish body length.

ROSY BARB • *Barbus conchonius*

This hardy little fish is ideal for beginners, as it is not fussy about water conditions (provided they do not become too warm) and will eat anything from algae and plants to flake, tablet, and live foods. Rosy barbs are peaceful and tolerant of other species and mix well with other similar-sized barbs. They are constantly on the move, so arrange the plants to allow space for this.

Young stock will not show the beautiful colors of the adults but appear silvery gold. It is not until they begin to mature that the males take on the red hues and the females become a deeper golden color. To ensure that you acquire both sexes, buy five or six youngsters or choose adult fish. If you want to see them at their best, be sure to keep both sexes so that the males display to the females.

Other forms
A long-finned form is available, but it is more demanding. Keep the temperature toward the upper end of the range. Be sure to maintain water quality and do not be tempted to overlook regular water changes.

▸ *Ideal conditions*

Water: Slightly acidic, slightly soft.
Temperature: 64-73°F (18-23°C).
Food: Small live or frozen aquatic invertebrates, such as daphnia, mosquito larvae, and bloodworm. Flake foods. Green foods.
Minimum number in the aquarium: 2.
Minimum tank size: 24 in (60 cm).
Tank region: Bottom, middle, and top.

Left: *Pairs of fish will break away from the shoal and spawn in the community aquarium – where the other inmates usually consider the eggs a free meal!*

Size: *Males and females 6 in (15 cm)*

The bright colors from which the rosy barb gets its common name develop as the fish matures.

▶ Origins

Streams, rivers, and pools in northern India, Assam, and Bengal.

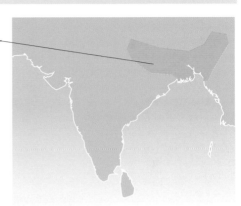

COPPER ROSY BARB
BARBUS CONCHONIUS
This farmed variant, measuring up to 6 in (15 cm), displays elongated finnage which, in some company, can turn it from a potential fin-worrier into a victim itself. Note the distinctive gold-edged black spot forward of the tail.

Female copper rosy barb.

▶ *Breeding*

Rosy barbs breed by scattering their eggs over fine-leaved plants. They can produce several hundred eggs but the parents will eat them, so remove the adults after spawning. It takes about 30 hours for the eggs to hatch, and the fry will feed greedily on fine foods.

Male copper rosy barb.

RUBY BARB • *Barbus nigrofasciatus*

The ruby barb's common name can be misleading, because it is only the male that exhibits the rich red color. The fish are also known as black ruby barbs and purple-headed barbs, so clearly the colors can vary! The colors are at their best when the males are ready to breed, so keep a group of both sexes.

You can keep these active little shoaling fish in a mixed shoal with other small barbs that have vertical stripes. They have no bad habits, other than occasionally nibbling at the plants, and will not harass other fish. Provide plenty of open water for them to swim in and use some broadleaved plants to create sheltered, dimly lit areas for them to retire to.

Conditioning

These fish benefit from a cooler spell during the winter months, when the tank temperature can be reduced to 68-72°F (20-22°C). This keeps them in good shape, especially for breeding. Return the temperature to the higher end of the range in summer. Do check that any other species in your aquarium can cope with this before you do it. The ruby barbs will not suffer if they are kept at a constant temperature, but they may not breed.

Breeding

Ruby barbs are egg-scatterers and the parents may eat their spawn, so remove them after spawning. The eggs hatch in 24 hours, and the fry take small live foods.

Size: *Males and females 2.4 in (6 cm)*

▶ Origins

Sluggish mountain streams in Sri Lanka.

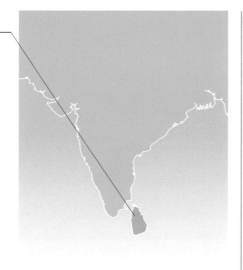

▶ *Ideal conditions*

Water: Slightly acidic to neutral, soft to slightly hard.
Temperature: 68-79°F (20-26°C).
Food: Small live or frozen aquatic invertebrates, such as daphnia, mosquito larvae, and bloodworm. Flake foods. A supply of green foods, such as peas and lettuce, deters the fish from eating plants.
Minimum number in the aquarium: 4.
Minimum tank size: 24 in (60 cm).
Tank region: Bottom, middle, and top.

BLACK-SPOT BARB
BARBUS FILAMENTOSUS

The black-spot is a beautiful barb measuring 6 in (15 cm), very active throughout the aquarium and worth considering as an alternative to the tiger barb if you are worried about the latter's potentially disruptive behavior. Juveniles have distinct two-bar markings on a gold background, as well as bright red flashes on the dorsal fin and tail lobes. As they grow, the fish lose the black bar through the middle of the body, but retain the black spot near the tail. Always look for examples with two black bars; being the younger fish, you can then enjoy watching their colors change as they mature. These peaceful barbs from India and Sri Lanka prefer the water to be slightly acid, but your aquarium shop should have specimens acclimatized to your local water conditions. These barbs create a better display as a group of six or more. Offer floating foods.

85

CHEQUER BARB • *Barbus oligolepis*

This little barb is useful for novice fishkeepers because it is easy to keep. Be sure to buy at least six of them because they really do like to be kept this way. It also ensures that you have both sexes. Males will sometimes spar with each other but very rarely do each other any damage. They are merely establishing their place within the shoal, as well as trying to entice willing females to spawn. Their sparring is not usually aimed at other tankmates. They like swimming space, so keep all plants to the sides and rear of the aquarium. They will eat just about anything they can get into their mouths and given a varied diet, these fish grow fast and can be sexually mature in less than six months.

Coloration

To see the iridescent sheen on the body, you must offer the fish some green foods, such as soft algae or lettuce and peas. A weekly feeding of live or frozen foods is also beneficial, especially if you are intending to breed the fish.

As the fish mature, the males develop more intense coloration and dark edges to their fins.

In females, the fins are iridescent yellow and do not develop dark margins as the fish matures.

Size: Males and females 3.5 in (9 cm)

Origins

Streams and rivers in most of Indonesia.

STRIPED BARB
BARBUS LINEATUS
Measuring 4.7 in (12 cm), males of this barb are slim and darkly pinstriped, while females are less distinctly marked, and much more rotund in their gravid (egg-carrying) state. This is quite an easy barb to spawn in plant thickets, and fry are numbered in thousands. (See pages 94-95 for more information on breeding barbs.)

The female has paler markings.

The male has a bolder pattern.

Ideal conditions

Water: Slightly acidic, slightly soft.
Temperature: 64-73°F (18-23°C).
Food: Small live or frozen aquatic invertebrates, such as daphnia, mosquito larvae, and bloodworm. Flake foods. Green foods.
Minimum number in the aquarium: 6.
Minimum tank size: 24 in (60 cm).
Tank region: Bottom and middle.

FIVE-BANDED BARB • *Barbus pentazona*

Five-banded barbs have not always been considered suitable fish for beginners. However, the fish imported today are often tank-raised and well acclimatized to aquarium conditions, so fishkeepers with a little experience could add them to their aquariums. You can overcome their natural timidity by keeping them in a well-planted aquarium that will provide cover should they feel threatened.

Like the majority of barbs, they prefer the company of their own kind, but they may also be combined with other peaceful species. As long as you keep them at the upper end of their temperature range and are able to provide a varied diet of live and/or frozen foods you should not have any problems. They are notorious for refusing to take flakes, but with tank-raised stock, this is proving to be less of a problem. They are difficult to breed, and the fry are hard to raise.

Below: *Males and females look very similar but they can be distinguished when they reach maturity. The males are slimmer and more brightly colored than the females.*

▶ **Origins**

Southeast Asia:
Malay Peninsula,
Singapore, and
Borneo.

ARULIUS BARB
BARBUS ARULIUS

The arulius barb from India is a sociable species that prefers to be kept in a small group. For this reason, and also because it is one of the bigger barb species, attaining a maximum adult size of 4.7 in (12 cm), it is best suited to the larger community tank. The arulius barb is placid, however, and can be kept with all but the smallest of tankmates. Males develop very elongated dorsal fin rays that add a different texture to the display. As the fish matures, the body develops a purple-blue color along the back, with black bars that act as part of the fish's natural camouflage. If the fish is not happy in the aquarium, the purple-blue fades to a dull grey. This robust and thickset fish is easy to spawn and unfussy about what it eats — including your soft-leaved aquarium plants! Live insect food is always welcome.

This purple color intensifies as the fish matures.

▶ *Ideal conditions*

Water: Slightly acidic to neutral, soft to slightly hard.
Temperature: 72-79°F (22-26°C).
Food: Small live or frozen aquatic invertebrates, such as daphnia, mosquito larvae, and bloodworm. Flake foods. Green foods.
Minimum number in the aquarium: 4.
Minimum tank size: 24 in (60 cm).
Tank region: Middle.

TIGER BARB • *Barbus tetrazona*

The tiger barb has a well-deserved reputation as a bully and a fin nipper. However, by understanding the needs of these highly attractive fish, it is possible to keep them without the usual chaos in the aquarium. The first thing to bear in mind is that they should be housed in large groups of at least eight specimens. They like to establish a pecking order within the shoal and, apart from the odd rogue fish, will normally be happily occupied maintaining this pecking order rather than nipping and harassing other tankmates. Choose these tankmates with utmost care. Avoid species that are slow moving or have long trailing fins, such as guppies, angelfish, Siamese fighting fish, and gouramis. Several variable color forms are available: albino, red, and green, but most retain the same nasty habits!

Mature males are slimmer, with more intense colors.

Ideal conditions

Water: Slightly acidic to neutral, soft to slightly hard.
Temperature: 68-79°F (20-26°C).
Food: Small live or frozen aquatic invertebrates, such as daphnia, mosquito larvae and bloodworm. Flake foods. Green foods.
Minimum number in the aquarium: 8.
Minimum tank size: 24 in (60 cm).
Tank region: Middle.

The color forms retain their markings, even though they may not be black bars.

Dark stars

Some aquarists like tiger barbs so much that they set up a special tank just for them. They can look quite stunning in an aquarium with a dark substrate, such as black gravel.

Size: Males and females 2.75 in (7 cm)

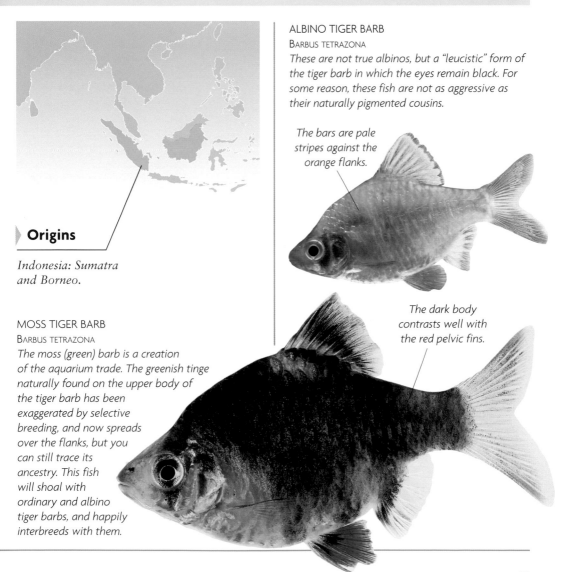

ALBINO TIGER BARB
BARBUS TETRAZONA

These are not true albinos, but a "leucistic" form of the tiger barb in which the eyes remain black. For some reason, these fish are not as aggressive as their naturally pigmented cousins.

The bars are pale stripes against the orange flanks.

▶ **Origins**

Indonesia: Sumatra and Borneo.

The dark body contrasts well with the red pelvic fins.

MOSS TIGER BARB
BARBUS TETRAZONA

The moss (green) barb is a creation of the aquarium trade. The greenish tinge naturally found on the upper body of the tiger barb has been exaggerated by selective breeding, and now spreads over the flanks, but you can still trace its ancestry. This fish will shoal with ordinary and albino tiger barbs, and happily interbreeds with them.

TWO-SPOT BARB or TICTO BARB • *Barbus ticto*

Two-spot barbs are often overlooked in dealers' tanks because they do not show their best colors until they are mature, and even then it can be difficult to tell males from females outside the breeding season. (Females do not usually have spots on their dorsal fins. Mature males are slimmer, have black spots on the edge of the dorsal fin, and a reddish band along the body.) However, it is well worth trying to keep these creatures, as they are probably one of the best small barbs for the community aquarium. They will quickly settle in a shoal with other small species, provided there is enough open water for them to do so.

Feed them plenty of frozen foods, such as bloodworm, or small live foods if you can get them, as well as flakes. A varied diet will help to produce healthy fish with good color.

Like any active fish, barbs can easily dislodge scales if they catch on sharp objects in the aquarium.

▶ *Ideal conditions*

Water: Slightly acidic to neutral, soft to slightly hard.
Temperature: 64-73°F (18-23°C).
Food: Small live or frozen aquatic invertebrates, such as daphnia, mosquito larvae, and bloodworm. Flake foods. Green foods.
Minimum number in the aquarium: 4.
Minimum tank size: 24 in (60 cm).
Tank region: Bottom, middle, and top.

Size: *Males and females 3 in (7.5 cm)*

▶ **Origins**

Rivers and streams in India and Sri Lanka to the Himalayas.

▶ *Breeding*

The fish breed in warmer water, with one male spawning with several females. The eggs are scattered over plants and hatch in 24 to 36 hours. The fry will take tiny foods.

GOLDEN BARB
BARBUS SEMIFASCIOLATUS
This color form of the olive-green species from southeastern China will feel at home among dense vegetation. Grouping together several cryptocoryne plants will achieve this effect in the aquarium. Keep this peaceful barb in a group of five or six individuals in any community aquarium. Maximum adult size: 4 in (10 cm).

CUMING'S BARB
BARBUS CUMINGI
These lively, peaceful fish do best in a small shoal and enjoy plenty of swimming space. They have a reticulated pattern on each scale, bright red dorsal and ventral fins, and two false eyespots on each side of the flanks that serve as a deterrent to predators in their natural Sri Lankan habitat. Since they remain relatively small, they suit any size of display. Maximum adult size: 2 in (5 cm).

CHERRY BARB • *Barbus titteya*

Cherry barbs are gregarious and popular little fish for the community aquarium that get their common name from the deep red color of the males. By contrast, the female is pale brown with a darker brown stripe that runs from the snout through the eye, along the body to the caudal peduncle. Bred by the thousands for the aquarium trade, the fish are now under threat in the wild.

Cherry barbs are very peaceful. They gather together in a shoal and then go their separate ways to rest quietly among the plants on their own. This is quite normal behavior. Young fish show little of the adult colors, but given plenty of frozen and live foods, supplemented with flakes (enriched with spirulina algae for color) and some green foods, they grow quickly.

Cherry barbs quickly settle to life in the community aquarium and can grow quite rapidly if well fed.

Size: Males and females 2 in (5 cm)

Origins

Shady streams and rivers in the lowlands of Sri Lanka.

Above: *Here, a ripe female cherry barb is about to spawn with her brighter-colored mate in dense vegetation.*

Ideal conditions

Water: Slightly acidic to neutral, soft to slightly hard.
Temperature: 73-79°F (23-26°C).
Food: Small live or frozen aquatic invertebrates, such as daphnia, mosquito larvae, and bloodworm. Flake foods. Green foods.
Minimum number in the aquarium: 4.
Minimum tank size: 18 in (45 cm).
Tank region: Bottom, middle, and top.

Sex differences

As they mature, males develop a beautiful bright scarlet color throughout most of the body.

Breeding

When breeding, the pair pass over fine-leaved plants, depositing one to three eggs at each pass. The eggs are clearly attached to the plants by a fine thread. The fish will lay as many as 300 eggs, but do beware: the parents will eat their eggs! The tiny fry hatch after 24 hours and will take fine live foods.

Bunches of fine-leaved plants.

Breeding setup

Position the tank in early morning sun.

Clean, slightly acidic water at 79-80°F (26-27°C).

PEARL DANIO • *Brachydanio albolineatus*

In the aquarium, these very active small fishes prefer a long tank where they can swim against a gentle current of water. Plant the aquarium along the back and sides, being sure to leave the main area open for the fish to swim. They are peaceful and may be kept with other similar-sized, placid species, such as some of the rasboras, other danios, and some of the smaller barbs. They are undemanding provided you remember to do regular water changes. Should you forget and the water quality drops, they may become sluggish and hide away or even refuse to feed. Normally, pearl danios greedily accept offerings of flakes, live, frozen, and freeze-dried foods; a mixed diet helps them retain their subtle coloration. They are ideal fish for beginners.

Breeding

All danios breed by scattering their eggs over plants. In warm, fresh water only 4-6 in (10-15 cm) deep, a trio of fish (two males and one female) will spawn over fine-leaved plants. Move the parents after spawning because they will eat the eggs. The eggs can take up to 48 hours to hatch and the fry need tiny live foods.

Females are deeper-bodied than the males.

The fine barbels can quickly deteriorate in poor conditions.

Size: Males and females 2.4 in (6 cm)

▶ Origins

Streams and rivers in Southeast Asia: Burma, Thailand, the Malay Peninsula, and Sumatra.

▶ *Ideal conditions*

Water: Slightly acidic to neutral, soft to slightly hard.
Temperature: 68-77°F (20-25°C).
Food: Small live or frozen aquatic invertebrates, such as daphnia, mosquito larvae, and bloodworm. Flake foods. Green foods.
Minimum number in the aquarium: 4.
Minimum tank size: 24 in (60 cm).
Tank region: Middle to top.

GOLD PEARL DANIO
Brachydanio albolineatus
Shown below is a golden variety of a fish that gives of its best when kept in large shoals. Fortunately, pearl danios are both inexpensive and hardy. In a group, both sexes show off their best coloration.

One of the main attractions of this species is the ever-changing delicate hues of color on the flanks. These are best seen when some light shines through the front glass of the aquarium. When lit from above, the effect is not so dramatic.

This farmed morph lacks the blue pigment of the wild fish but, to compensate, the finnage is attractively banded in orange.

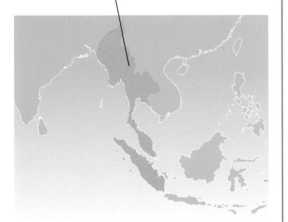

ZEBRA DANIO • *Brachydanio rerio*

When you see the deep blue and gold stripes along the body of mature healthy specimens, you will agree that the common name zebra danio is an obvious choice for these highly popular aquarium fish. (An albino form and a long-finned variety are also available.) Do not, however, expect to see this coloration in the shop, where young fish may look a little pale. Given a varied diet that includes some live or frozen foods, they soon develop into good-quality adults. A shoal is constantly on the move around the tank but blends well with species of similar temperament.

It is not easy to distinguish the sexes in young stock, but mature males have more intense coloration and are slimmer than females. In a group of four fish, you should end up with at least one pair, but to increase the chances, buy six. This is the perfect beginner's fish and probably the first egglayer that fishkeepers try to spawn at home.

Allow the fish plenty of swimming space. Thickets of plants will provide hiding places should the fish need them.

Ideal conditions

Water: Slightly acidic to neutral, soft to slightly hard.
Temperature: 64-75°F (18-24°C).
Food: Small live or frozen aquatic invertebrates, such as daphnia, mosquito larvae, and bloodworm.
Flake foods.
Green foods and algae.
Minimum number in the aquarium: 4.
Minimum tank size: 24 in (60 cm).
Tank region: Middle to top.

In good-quality fish, the lines along the flanks are unbroken.

Size: *Males and females 2.4 in (6 cm)*

▶ Origins

Eastern India,
from Calcutta
to Masulipatam.

Below: *Although superficially different, the leopard (top) and zebra danio are the same species and are sexed in the same way.*

▶ *Breeding*

Zebra danios are easy to breed, provided the fish are allowed to pair themselves from the shoal and are well fed on live foods to bring them into breeding condition. Adding cold water to the tank triggers spawning. A full-grown pair will scatter up to 500 eggs over plants. These hatch in about 48 hours; provide commercial fry foods, as well as tiny live foods.

Breeding setup

Fine-leaved plants and some gentle aeration.

Set the temperature at 73-79°F (23-26°C).

Tank measuring 24x12x12 in (60x30x30 cm).

Large pea gravel or a double layer of glass marbles.

GIANT DANIO • *Danio aequipinnatus*

The giant danio is always on the move, so much so that it could be described as restless. It is quite tolerant of other fish, but never keep it with anything that may harass or intimidate it. Some of the larger rainbowfish, for example, would compete for the same swimming space. Keep any planting to the rear and sides of the tank and allow one or two broadleaved plants (such as Amazon swordplants) to reach the surface so that the fish can retire between the leaves. Such cover also helps to deter these athletic fish from jumping out of the aquarium.

Safety first

The giant danio requires space and a quiet aquarium, as it is easily frightened and will readily jump to avoid potential danger. Use a cover glass!

The color and markings on these fish can vary depending on the quality of the breeding stock – something over which we have little control.

▶ Ideal conditions

Water: Slightly acidic to neutral, soft to slightly hard.
Temperature: 72-75°F (22-24°C).
Food: Small live or frozen aquatic invertebrates, such as daphnia, mosquito larvae, and bloodworm. Flake foods. Green foods. Be sure to offer a varied diet.
Minimum number in the aquarium: 4.
Minimum tank size: 30 in (75 cm).
Tank region: Middle to top.

▶ Breeding

Males are slimmer than females. Giant danios lay their eggs on plants over a period of time; each time the pair come together about 8-10 eggs are laid, and this process continues until the female is spent. By this time, a full-grown pair may have produced as many as 300 eggs. Move the parents after spawning and the eggs will hatch in around 36 hours. Feed the fry on small live foods.

Size: *Males and females 4 in (10 cm)*

▶ Origins

Streams and
pools on the
west coast
of India and
Sri Lanka.

In males (shown
here) the central
blue band
continues straight
into the tail; in
females, it turns
upward.

GOLD GIANT DANIO
DANIO AEQUIPINNATUS
*The lively gold giant danios lack the
blue pigment of the normal form. Their
coloration is the result of selective
breeding. They also grow to 4 in (10 cm).*

*Both the giant danio and the Bengal
danio (Danio devario) are suited to larger,
planted aquariums, and are fishes of
running, rather than stagnant, water.
Provide good aeration.*

*Top-swimming fishes in the Cyprinidae
family add liveliness to the aquarium. Their
slender bodies indicate that they are fast
swimmers, often just as at home in a
mountain stream as in the slower-moving
waters of the jungle. These fishes have no
teeth in their jaws, but they do have teeth
in the throat to grind up their food.*

*Gold giant danios glow
under tank lights.*

WHITE CLOUD MTN MINNOW ● *Tanichthys albonubes*

This colorful little fish is often overlooked because of its small size, but if you only have room for a small tank, it should be top of your list. The main thing to remember is that White Clouds cannot stand too much warmth for a protracted period of time.

White Clouds like a tank with thickets of plants for shelter and the company of their own kind, so be sure to keep them in a shoal of at least six. If these conditions are not met, the fish will become very timid and sulk in the corner of the tank, while their beautiful colors pale into insignificance.

Other forms

A long-finned variety is also available. It is more trouble to keep, as it requires slightly warmer tank conditions, otherwise it may suffer from bacterial infections.

Males, as here, are more colorful, slim fish, while the females are more rounded.

Left: *Even in the community aquarium, White Cloud Mountain minnows will come into spawning condition. If you are lucky, you can watch the males court and spawn with the well-rounded females (shown here).*

Size: Males and females 1.6 in (4 cm)

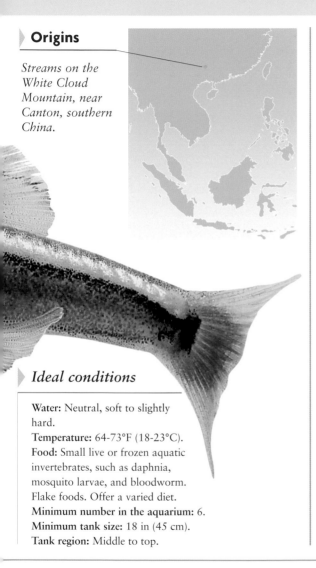

Origins

Streams on the White Cloud Mountain, near Canton, southern China.

Ideal conditions

Water: Neutral, soft to slightly hard.
Temperature: 64-73°F (18-23°C).
Food: Small live or frozen aquatic invertebrates, such as daphnia, mosquito larvae, and bloodworm. Flake foods. Offer a varied diet.
Minimum number in the aquarium: 6.
Minimum tank size: 18 in (45 cm).
Tank region: Middle to top.

Breeding White Clouds

The male courts his chosen female, spreading his fins and swimming around her until the pair come together and swim over some fine-leaved plants, shedding spawn and milt (sperm). The eggs hatch after 36 hours, and the fry need fine live foods. These fish are so easy to breed in cool conditions that many aquarists put them outside during the warm summer months and find that the fish breed readily in plant-filled ponds and tubs.

Above: *With the aquarium lights on, the full beauty of the White Cloud Mountain minnow soon becomes apparent.*

HARLEQUIN • *Rasbora heteromorpha*

In a tank with planted areas and some open water, harlequins will have room to swim as well as quieter, dimly lit areas beneath the plants to which they can retire. Harlequins like the company of their own kind but will also shoal with other rasboras and danios. Most beginners want to add this very popular aquarium fish to the tank straightaway, but patience is the key. Make sure that your tank has settled down and that you have started to master water changes, filter cleaning, feeding, etc. Wait six to nine months before you try keeping these fish; otherwise they will quickly perish. On a varied diet that includes small frozen and even live foods, the fish will be more robust and have much better color. Regular water changes are essential to keep them healthy.

Below: This is a typical female harlequin, showing a deeper body outline than the male. The bold markings and iridescent fins of these fish provide a striking display in the home community aquarium.

Size: Males and females 1.8 in (4.5 cm)

▶ Origins

Southeast Asia:
Malay Peninsula
and Northeast
Sumatra.

Left: *Harlequins
invert in order to
lay their eggs on
the underside of
broadleaved plants.*

▶ *Ideal conditions*

Water: Slightly acidic to neutral,
soft to slightly hard.
Temperature: 72-77°F (22-25°C).
Food: Small live or frozen aquatic
invertebrates, such as daphnia,
mosquito larvae, and bloodworm.
Flake foods.
Minimum number in the aquarium: 8.
Minimum tank size: 18 in (45 cm).
Tank region: Middle to top.

Breeding rasboras

*Place a well-conditioned adult male with
a younger plump female in the aquarium
late in the evening. Courtship is instigated
by the male and includes fin-flaring and
dancing in front of his intended mate.
The pair start swimming around the tank
together and eventually move underneath
a suitable leaf. Here, they turn upside
down and deposit a few eggs. Then they
move off and court some more before
coming back to spawn again (usually in
the same general area). About 40 eggs are
deposited in an average spawning.
Remove the parents from the spawning
tank. The eggs hatch the following day
and fry are free swimming on the third
day. Feed them infusoria or liquid fry
foods for a week before offering them
brine shrimp. They grow very quickly,
reaching 1 in (2.5 cm) in only three months.*

*In females, the
dark marking has
a straight
edge.*

*In males, the leading
edge is sloped.*

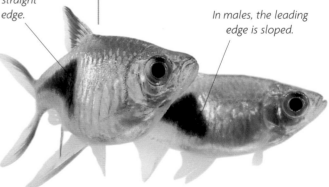

REDLINE RASBORA • *Rasbora pauciperforata*

Often overlooked in dealers' tanks because of its lack of color, this lively little rasbora quickly settles into an aquarium and, if fed a wide variety of foods, soon develops a bold red line along its flanks. These peaceful shoaling fish feel safe in a group of at least four and happily coexist with other midwater-swimming fishes of a similar size.

Carrying out regular water changes is essential, otherwise these fish will suffer. If you notice them sulking away in a corner or just lurking in the plants, their color faded and their fins clamped, this is a sure sign that there is a potential problem. Take prompt action; something as simple as a water change will usually correct the conditions, and the fish will soon be out and about again.

⟩ *Ideal conditions*

Water: Slightly acidic to neutral, soft to slightly hard.
Temperature: 73-77°F (23-25°C).
Food: Live or frozen small aquatic invertebrates, such as daphnia, mosquito larvae, and bloodworm. Flake foods. The fish also enjoy grazing on soft algae and lettuce.
Minimum number in the aquarium: 4
Minimum tank size: 24 in (60 cm).
Tank region: Middle to top.

These fish relish small live foods.

Size: Males and females 2.75 in (7 cm)

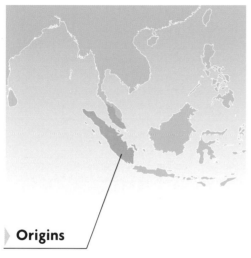

▶ Origins

Southeast Asia:
western Malaysia
and Sumatra.

▶ Breeding

Males are generally slimmer than females. These egglayers are notoriously difficult to breed because they are selective about their partners. If you do have a compatible pair, they will lay their eggs among fine-leaved plants. Hatching takes about 24 hours, and the fry require very small foods.

RED-TAILED RASBORA
RASBORA BORAPETENSIS

In an aquarium with open water areas, these small shoaling fish from southeastern Thailand like being kept with similar species, such as the zebra danio. With plants around the sides and back and low-growing plants toward the front, red-tailed rasboras will happily dart among the plants to swim around with the other fish. Red-tailed rasboras are not easy to sex, especially as youngsters, but because you will be buying a group of them, there is every chance that it will contain at least one fish of each sex. As the fish grow up, males will become recognizable as slimmer than the deep-bodied females. Frozen daphnia and bloodworm in the diet help to maintain the beautiful iridescent sheen on the body.

SCISSORTAIL • *Rasbora trilineata*

Scissortails are among the larger rasboras, so keep them in a long aquarium with plenty of swimming space. Position plants to the back and sides to provide cover should they be scared; this will help to curb their desire to jump out of danger! They like a tank with a gentle current of water to swim against. Regular water changes are essential.

These fish are no trouble at all to feed. They take flake foods from the surface and such is their eagerness to feed that they will sometimes flip out of the water. Remember that a varied diet makes for a healthier fish, so do offer alternative foods, such as frozen bloodworm and live foods.

Scissortails can be susceptible to white spot if conditions are not quite right, if there is a sudden change of temperature or if they are stressed by inappropriate tankmates. Do not keep them with larger fish that may harass them.

▶ *Ideal conditions*

Water: Slightly acidic to neutral, soft to slightly hard.
Temperature: 73-77°F (23-25°C).
Food: Small live or frozen aquatic invertebrates, such as daphnia, mosquito larvae, and bloodworm. Flake foods.
Minimum number in the aquarium: 4.
Minimum tank size: 24 in (60 cm).
Tank region: Middle to top.

Safety first

These lively, active fish tend to jump when frightened, so do not forget to put a cover glass on the tank.

These fish can easily damage their bodies when jumping.

Size: *Males and females 6 in (15 cm)*

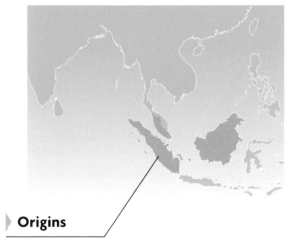

CLOWN RASBORA
RASBORA KALOCHROMA

This sleek little fish, with its distinctive black spot marking, adds finesse to the display. It may reach a maximum adult size of 4 in (10 cm), but is rarely more than 2.75-3.2 in (7-8 cm). However, the lovely clown rasboras can become a little possessive of a particular area within the aquarium. The solution is to keep them in a group of six or more with plenty of other fish, so that they do not get a chance to set up a territory. Their natural home is in Malaysia, Sumatra and Borneo and they prefer well-planted surroundings in which they can shelter from bright lighting.

▶ **Origins**

The lakes, rivers, and streams of western Malaysia, Sumatra and Borneo.

Right: *The small but colorful clown rasbora adds interest to the community aquarium.*

FLYING FOX • *Epalzeorhynchus kalopterus*

Once your aquarium has settled down, the flying fox is a useful fish for picking away at algae, but it will not eat thread algae; you will have to get rid of that yourself! It will also eat planarian worms, which makes it a useful biological control, preferable to treating the aquarium with chemicals to get rid of these pests. However, these eating habits do not mean that you need not feed the fish; they will take flake, tablet, and granular foods, but relish live and green foods.

Flying foxes can be territorial, so keep just one in a 24 in (60 cm) tank; otherwise they will pick on each other, which could result in the death of the weaker fish. This aside, they are quite endearing characters that spend a lot of time resting on their pectoral fins on leaves or rocks. In a planted aquarium with well-oxygenated water, you will often see them "playing" in the outflow from the filter system. Keep the tank covered; flying foxes are notorious jumpers! Regular water changes and efficient filtration are essential to keep them healthy.

Ideal conditions

Water: Slightly acidic to neutral, soft to slightly hard.
Temperature: 75-79°F (24-26°C).
Food: Small live or frozen aquatic invertebrates, such as daphnia, mosquito larvae, and bloodworm. Flake foods. Green foods.
Maximum number in a 24 in (60 cm) aquarium: 1. More in a larger tank.
Minimum tank size: 24 in (60 cm).
Tank region: Bottom to middle.

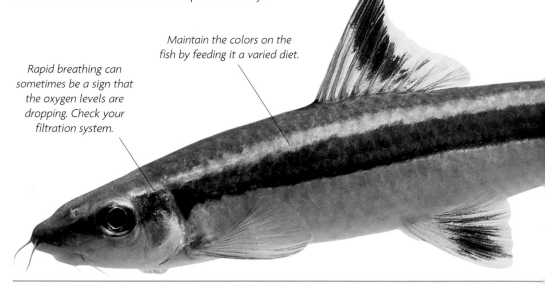

Maintain the colors on the fish by feeding it a varied diet.

Rapid breathing can sometimes be a sign that the oxygen levels are dropping. Check your filtration system.

Size: *Males and females 6 in (15 cm)*

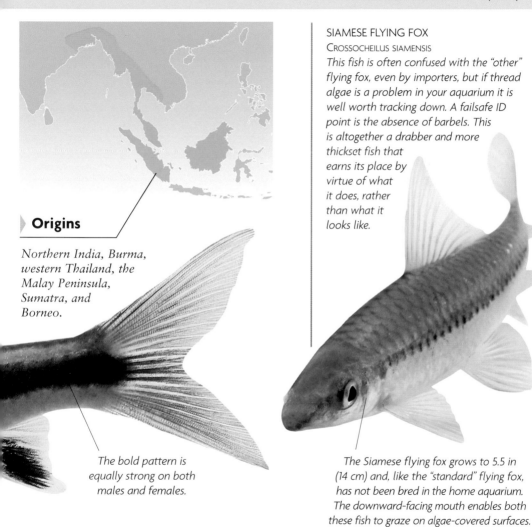

SIAMESE FLYING FOX
CROSSOCHEILUS SIAMENSIS

This fish is often confused with the "other" flying fox, even by importers, but if thread algae is a problem in your aquarium it is well worth tracking down. A failsafe ID point is the absence of barbels. This is altogether a drabber and more thickset fish that earns its place by virtue of what it does, rather than what it looks like.

▶ **Origins**

Northern India, Burma, western Thailand, the Malay Peninsula, Sumatra, and Borneo.

The bold pattern is equally strong on both males and females.

The Siamese flying fox grows to 5.5 in (14 cm) and, like the "standard" flying fox, has not been bred in the home aquarium. The downward-facing mouth enables both these fish to graze on algae-covered surfaces.

RED-TAILED BLACK SHARK • *Epalzeorhynchos bicolor*

The red-tailed black shark is a popular fish due to its striking colors and, of course, its "sharklike" finnage. However, the RTBS, as it is often referred to, is not without its drawbacks. If added early on in the stocking stages of a community aquarium, it will consider the aquarium its own and aggressively chase other fish. Vicious squabbles are inevitable if one RTBS is kept with another RTBS or the closely related ruby shark. Even in established tanks, an RTBS can "turn" and become problematic. For these reasons, the RTBS is best kept with tough fishes such as medium-large barbs, larger tetras, catfish, and rainbowfish. The RTBS does have its uses though; it is an excellent scavenger and grazer and can remove the toughest of algae if no other food is available.

Few fish can boast the solid contrasting colors of the RTBS, along with its striking body shape.

The sensitive barbels and strong mouth of a superb scavenger.

▶ *Ideal conditions*

Water: Soft to medium-hard. Neutral.
Temperature: 72-79°F (22-26°C).
Food: Sinking foods including pellets, wafers, and frozen or live foods.
Minimum number in the aquarium: Only one per tank.
Minimum tank size: 36 in (90 cm).
Tank region: Bottom.

The RTBS will appreciate its own hiding spots among plants, roots, or a cave.

Size: Males and females 5 in (13 cm)

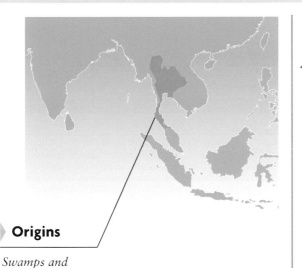

Origins

Swamps and streams in Thailand

RUBY SHARK

EPALZEORHYNCHOS FRENATUS

Closely related to the RTBS, the ruby, or red-finned, shark is marginally thinner in shape and somewhat better behaved. When young, these fish have a stunning black body with bright red fins, but over time, the body color will fade to a misty charcoal-grey. As this happens, a black facial stripe running from the back of the eye to the mouth and a black spot at the base of the tail become visible.

The caudal spot is just visible.

ALBINO SHARK

EPALZEORHYNCHOS FRENATUS

The albino shark is the albino variety of the ruby shark. Both fish grow to 6 in (15 cm) and require similar conditions to the RTBS. In true albinism there is a complete lack of the black pigment, melanin, and the eyes are red. In this example you can still detect faint traces of the caudal spot. True albinos seldom reach maturity in the wild because they are too conspicuous.

CONGO TETRA ● *Phenacogrammus interruptus*

The Congo tetra is one of the most impressive medium-sized characins. The fish love to swim, so allow for this by careful planting that gives them plenty of open water to move about in. They are susceptible to disease if water conditions deteriorate, so do not forget the water changes! Feeding is simple; they will eat dried foods but, to maintain the body sheen, be sure to include live foods or their frozen equivalents. Congos can be nervous, especially if you try keeping them in small numbers; they need the security of the shoal. Avoid keeping them with fish that are likely to nibble their finnage.

The clearly visible scales and intense coloration add to the charm of these creatures.

Compatibility

Male Congo tetras can be quarrelsome with each other, so do not try to crowd them in the aquarium.

Ideal conditions

Water: Slightly acidic to neutral, slightly soft.
Temperature: 72-79°F (22-26°C).
Food: Small live or frozen aquatic invertebrates, such as daphnia, mosquito larvae, and bloodworm. Flake foods.
Minimum number in the aquarium: 6.
Minimum tank size: 36 in (90 cm).
Tank region: Middle.

Mature males are easy to distinguish by their extended finnage and ragged-looking caudal fin.

Origins

The Zaire River and nearby lakes in Central Africa.

Size: Males 3.3 in (8.5 cm), females 2.4 in (6 cm)

▶ *Breeding*

Place a well-conditioned pair of Congo tetras in a breeding tank shortly before turning out the lights. Most pairs will spawn the following morning. The clear eggs adhere to plant fronds or a spawning mop or fall into the peat substrate, and the large eggs hatch out in about five days.

Rearing the fry

Fry hang on to the spawning medium for a couple of days before they become free swimming. At this time they need infusoria for a day or two before tackling newly hatched brine shrimp. Once the fry are 0.8 in (2 cm) long, they will take larger foods and a proprietary growth food. They are sexable at 2 in (5 cm), but are nearer 3 in (7.5 cm) before they are sexually mature.

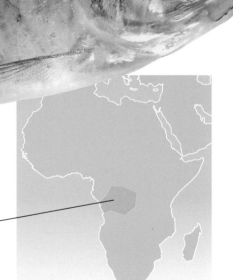

Very soft water at pH 6.5 and 77°F (25°C).

Tank measuring 36x12x18 in (90x30x45 cm).

Alternatively, use spawning mops.

Provide Java moss as a spawning medium.

Waterlogged peat substrate.

SILVER-TIPPED TETRA ● *Hasemania nana*

The silver-tipped tetra, so-called because of the light tips to its fins, is well-suited to a community aquarium of peaceful fishes (although it can be "nippy"). In typical tetra fashion, it shoals in vast numbers in patches of open water and seeks refuge among plants when danger threatens. It will patrol the middle layer of the aquarium. In the wild, it inhabits small streams with a good flow of highly oxygenated water. Accordingly, you should plant the aquarium with thickets of plants and leave some open areas. Ensure that the aquarium filtration system is working efficiently and providing a good supply of well-oxygenated water. Being quite robust, it is one of the first characins that you can add to a community tank about a month after adding your first fish.

▌ *Ideal conditions*

Water: Slightly acidic to neutral, soft to slightly hard.
Temperature: 72-82°F (22-28°C).
Food: Small live or frozen aquatic invertebrates, such as daphnia, mosquito larvae, and bloodworm. Flake foods. Provide a varied diet.
Minimum number in the aquarium: 4.
Minimum tank size: 24 in (60 cm).
Tank region: Middle.

Size: Males and females 2 in (5 cm)

▶ Origins

Eastern Brazil,
River Sao Francisco
basin; western
Brazil, in the
tributaries of the
River Purus.

WHITE-SPOT TETRA
APHYOCHARAX PARAGUAYENSIS

This species, from the Paraguay Basin, carries its telltale white spots at the base of the tail, together with a flash on the anal fin. Its delicate silver color makes a good contrast to neon and cardinal tetras in the community aquarium. The white-spot (or dawn) tetra prefers slightly acidic water and is one of the more sensitive tetra species. It is not hardy enough to be recommended as one of the first fish to add to a display; wait until the water conditions have matured. It grows to a mature size of 1.8 in (4.5 cm).

▶ Breeding

These little egglayers will produce about 300 eggs but take care – the parents will eat the eggs. For first foods, offer newly hatched brine shrimp and, as the fish grow, increase the size of the live foods.

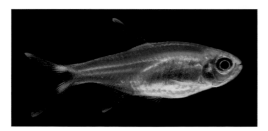

Left: *Females are more yellow in color than the orange males, with less brightly marked tips to the fins. Mature males (main photograph) appear slimmer than females and have striking white tips to the dorsal, anal, and caudal fins.*

GLOWLIGHT • *Hemigrammus erythrozonus*

FAMILY: CHARACIDAE (CHARACINS)

Glowlights are bred by the thousand on fish farms, just for the tropical fish industry. The majority of fish we buy now are raised in this way and have been acclimatized to suit the conditions found in the average community aquarium. They are, therefore, an excellent choice for the novice fishkeeper. Buy a small shoal, feed them well, and they will reward you with good color and plenty of activity. The origin of the common name is obvious – the bright red line that runs the length of the fish.

Although glowlights will accept all the usual small aquarium foods, you do need to pay some attention to the feeding regimen. The fish prefer to be fed small amounts two or three times a day, rather than a single meal in the morning or evening, although they will survive on this. The little-and-often feeding regimen really comes into play if you wish to bring them into breeding condition.

Ideal conditions

Water: Slightly acidic to neutral, soft to slightly hard.
Temperature: 73-82°F (23-28°C).
Food: Small live or frozen aquatic invertebrates, such as daphnia, mosquito larvae, and bloodworm. Flake foods.
Minimum number in the aquarium: 4.
Minimum tank size: 24 in (60 cm).
Tank region: Middle.

Below: *Contented fish display their color and finnage to full advantage.*

Size: Males and females 1.6 in (4 cm)

▶ Origins

Guyana: in the Essequibo River.

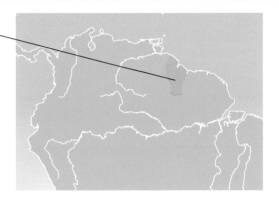

Left: Carefully check the fish you buy. Due to inbreeding, they can sometimes exhibit deformities, unlike this good-looking fish.

Below: The glowlight tetra adds a brilliant flash of orange-pink to the aquarium display, leading newcomers to believe that these fish somehow generate their own light. This convincing illusion probably assists shoals of glowlights to stay close-knit in the sun-dappled waters of their tropical Guyanan home.

▶ *Breeding*

Males are slimmer than females. Breeding is typical of the tetras, with the eggs being scattered over plants. Feed the fry regular small feeds of tiny live foods.

HEAD AND TAIL LIGHT • *Hemigrammus ocellifer*

You can almost see right through the body wall of this small characin. In fact, this helps you to distinguish the sexes, because in males the silvery swimbladder appears more pointed, while in females it is more rounded. The head and tail light is a good addition to the community aquarium, peaceful both with its own kind and with other fish. It spends much of its time among plants where it feels safe, but drop in the food and it is one of the first to get to it. Live foods bring out the best colors, but if these are not available, offer the fish a good varied diet of frozen and flake foods.

Be sure to carry out regular water changes and check that the filtration system is working efficiently, as the fish like well-oxygenated, clean water. The water changes will also help to prevent a buildup of nitrates, which the fish will not tolerate.

▶ Breeding

An easy characin to breed. In soft, acidic, warm conditions, the fish will scatter their eggs over fine-leaved plants. Raise the fry on newly hatched brine shrimp.

The larger the shoal, the more willing the head and tail light is to venture out into the aquarium.

Size: Males and females 2 in (5 cm)

▶ Origins

The Guianas and northern Amazon Basin.

▶ *Ideal conditions*

Water: Slightly acidic to neutral, soft to slightly hard.
Temperature: 72-82°F (22-28°C).
Food: Small live or frozen aquatic invertebrates, such as daphnia, mosquito larvae, and bloodworm. Flake foods.
Minimum number in the aquarium: 4.
Minimum tank size: 24 in (60 cm).
Tank region: Middle.

Creating a peat substrate

Left: Crumble a 2 in (5 cm)-thick layer of peat onto the water surface. Use rainwater filtered through carbon or reverse osmosis water mixed with tapwater to achieve the correct hardness.

Left: The peat will initially float on the surface and may take a week or so to sink to the bottom. Stirring it every day and squeezing pieces that are full of air helps to make it sink more quickly.

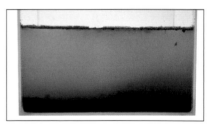

Above: The water is now acidified and contains many beneficial trace elements. You can siphon it into another container for use with those fish that require soft, acidic water or use the tank as it is.

BLEEDING HEART TETRA • *Hyphessobrycon erythrostigma*

This brightly colored tetra is often overlooked because it fails to show its true colors in the shop tank. Very young specimens also lack the elongated dorsal and anal finnage seen in adult males. But try them. The delicate pinkish red body color, and the distinctive red "heart" mark on the flanks make them worthwhile. The fish normally available are wild caught and can be difficult to acclimatize, so check that they have been in the shop for a while and are feeding well. Take care over water quality and carry out regular water changes to avoid any buildup of nitrates. Once established in the aquarium, they will feed readily on flake but benefit greatly from regular supplies of frozen and live foods in their diet.

Compatibility

The bleeding heart tetra prefers to be kept with other smaller, peaceful fishes. In the company of boisterous tank mates it just hides among the plants. Unusually for a tetra, you can keep a large group of these fish or just a pair, provided the pair have other tetras to swim with.

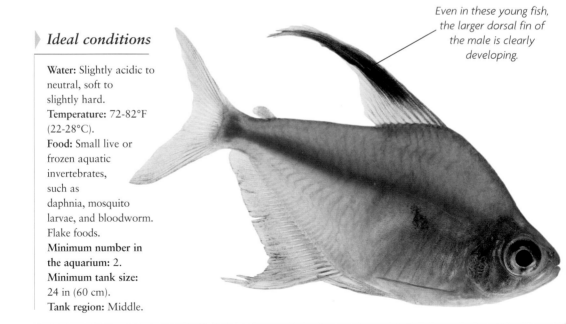

Even in these young fish, the larger dorsal fin of the male is clearly developing.

▷ *Ideal conditions*

Water: Slightly acidic to neutral, soft to slightly hard.
Temperature: 72-82°F (22-28°C).
Food: Small live or frozen aquatic invertebrates, such as daphnia, mosquito larvae, and bloodworm. Flake foods.
Minimum number in the aquarium: 2.
Minimum tank size: 24 in (60 cm).
Tank region: Middle.

Size: Males and females 2.4 in (6 cm)

Origins

Amazon Basin in Peru and western Brazil.

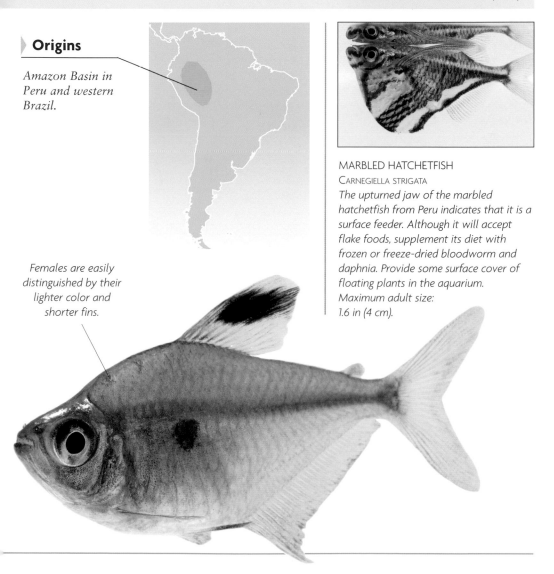

MARBLED HATCHETFISH
CARNEGIELLA STRIGATA
The upturned jaw of the marbled hatchetfish from Peru indicates that it is a surface feeder. Although it will accept flake foods, supplement its diet with frozen or freeze-dried bloodworm and daphnia. Provide some surface cover of floating plants in the aquarium. Maximum adult size: 1.6 in (4 cm).

Females are easily distinguished by their lighter color and shorter fins.

123

BLACK NEON ● *Hyphessobrycon herbertaxelrodi*

The black neon is another little characin that is farmed to supply the hobby. Wild-caught fish are very demanding in terms of water conditions, but farmed fish are much more tolerant – so much so that they can easily be kept in a community aquarium. Do not add them as starter fish, but after a month to six weeks they will be able to live quite happily in your aquarium, provided you are keeping other peaceful species.

Black neons are typical shoaling fish, spending some time hanging in the water just flicking their fins every now and then before swimming off for a while and then retiring to the plants.

Below: *The fish should show good color and swim with their fins erect. If not, check the water conditions, and rectify them if necessary.*

Ideal conditions

Water: Slightly acidic to neutral, soft to slightly hard.
Temperature: 72-82°F (22-28°C).
Food: Small live or frozen aquatic invertebrates, such as daphnia, mosquito larvae, and bloodworm. Flake foods. A varied diet is vital to bring the fish into breeding condition.
Minimum number in the aquarium: 4.
Minimum tank size: 24 in (60 cm).
Tank region: Middle.

Size: Males and females 1.6 in (4 cm)

Right: *In black neons the top half of the eye has a distinctive red marking.*

▶ Origins

The Mato Grosso region of Brazil, in the Taquari River.

▶ Breeding

Adult males are slimmer than the females. They breed in soft acid water, scattering their eggs over fine-leaved plants. The eggs hatch in about 36 hours; feed the fry tiny live foods such as newly hatched brine shrimp.

BLACK PHANTOM TETRA • *Megalamphodus megalopterus*

This small, predominantly black characin will add a little contrast to your aquarium. Given good water quality, including low nitrate levels, it is also one of the easiest tetras to maintain in captivity. It does not look its best in a dealer's tank; it requires the security of a well-planted aquarium and good feeding to settle down and show its true colors.

In the wild it is found in shady streams, so provide a tank with some planting, some open areas and a gentle current of water flowing through it. Choose companion fish with care. They should be peaceful and not the type to nip another fish's fins. The black phantom's large fins can be just too much of a temptation to some fish. Females show more red in their fins.

▶ Ideal conditions

Water: Slightly acidic to neutral, soft to slightly hard.
Temperature: 64-82°F (18-28°C).
Food: Small live or frozen aquatic invertebrates, such as daphnia, mosquito larvae, and bloodworm. Flake foods.
Minimum number in the aquarium: 2.
Minimum tank size: 24 in (60 cm).
Tank region: Middle.

Size: Males and females 1.8 in (4.5 cm)

▶ Origins

In the River Sao Francisco, eastern Brazil.

Below: The male is dark grey with black fins and a larger dorsal fin.

▶ Breeding

Given a varied diet, the fish will come into breeding condition, and it is not unusual to see pairs displaying in the community aquarium. They are egg scatterers and can be bred in soft, acidic conditions with subdued lighting. Feed the fry tiny live foods.

RED PHANTOM TETRA
MEGALAMPHODUS SWEGLESI

The red phantom tetra from Colombia is a close cousin of the black phantom, featuring similar black markings but on a red background. It is more delicate than the black phantom and requires very good conditions to do well. However, the effort is worthwhile, as the fish will reward you with its stunning red hues and placid behavior. The red phantom should be one of the last fish you add to your display, as all the aquarium conditions need to be as stable as possible before you introduce it. The red phantom looks best in a small shoal of six to eight individuals. It grows to a maximum adult size of 1.8 in (4.5 cm). Avoid keeping it with larger, potentially aggressive fish.

Below: *This young red phantom tetra is typical of those available in dealers' tanks. The full color and pattern will develop with maturity.*

DIAMOND TETRA • *Moenkhausia pitteri*

Diamond tetras will flourish in a peaceful, planted community aquarium. If possible, provide a gentle flow of water through the tank. A group of young fish, which are often overlooked in dealers' tanks, because they have none of the flamboyant features of the adults, will quickly mature if fed a diet that incorporates plenty of small, live, or frozen aquatic invertebrates. They accept flake food, but feeding the fish on this diet alone usually results in fish that lack the added sparkle.

Ideal conditions

Water: Soft, slightly acidic.
Temperature: 75-82°F (24-28°C).
Food: Small live or frozen aquatic invertebrates, such as daphnia, mosquito larvae, and bloodworm. Flake foods.
Minimum number in the aquarium: 6.
Minimum tank size: 24 in (60 cm).
Tank region: Middle.

A well-rounded female specimen such as this will raise the fins of any male diamond tetra.

Compatibility
Be careful not to keep diamond tetras with fish species that may nibble their fins.

Correct feeding and water conditions will help maintain the intense coloration and sparkle of the male fish.

Size: *Males and females 2.5 in (6.5 cm)*

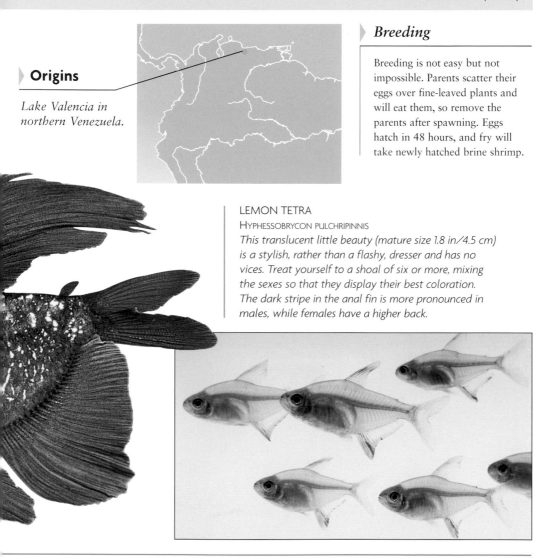

Origins

Lake Valencia in northern Venezuela.

Breeding

Breeding is not easy but not impossible. Parents scatter their eggs over fine-leaved plants and will eat them, so remove the parents after spawning. Eggs hatch in 48 hours, and fry will take newly hatched brine shrimp.

LEMON TETRA

HYPHESSOBRYCON PULCHRIPINNIS

This translucent little beauty (mature size 1.8 in/4.5 cm) is a stylish, rather than a flashy, dresser and has no vices. Treat yourself to a shoal of six or more, mixing the sexes so that they display their best coloration. The dark stripe in the anal fin is more pronounced in males, while females have a higher back.

CARDINAL TETRA ● *Paracheirodon axelrodi*

The brilliant colors of this characin make it one of the most popular aquarium fish, but it is not one of the easiest to keep. Do not introduce it into a newly set up aquarium but wait until your system has settled down and see what the water parameters average out at. (This is one good reason for keeping an aquarium log!) You will need soft, slightly acidic conditions and a mature tank with well-established thickets of plants to provide shelter. It is well worth saving up to buy a shoal of these fish. Single fish tend to hide away, as do two or three, but they gain strength in numbers and will also look far more impressive. The vast majority of cardinals offered for sale are wild caught and highly sought-after community fish.

Ideal conditions

Water: Slightly acidic, soft.
Temperature: 73-80°F (23-27°C).
Food: Tiny live or frozen aquatic invertebrates, such as daphnia, mosquito larvae, and bloodworm that the fish can take with their small mouths. Flake foods.
Minimum number in the aquarium: 6.
Minimum tank size: 24 in (60 cm).
Tank region: Middle.

Size: Males and females 2 in (5 cm)

▶ Origins

Northwestern Brazil.

Cardinal tetras caused a stir when they were first imported into the USA in 1956, soon challenging neons for the title of most popular tropical aquarium fish. Red belly, blue iridescent stripe, white-bordered dorsal and anal fins, and prominent eyes, luminescent under artificial light and peaceful, too – quite a combination! The bigger the shoal, the better the effect, especially against a dark background.

Cardinal tetra (Paracheirodon axelrodi)

Neon tetra (Paracheirodon innesi)

▶ Breeding

Although the cardinal is an egg layer and has been bred, it is not easy to do, as they are extremely particular about water parameters. They can produce up to 500 eggs, and the fry need very small live foods. It is worth noting that if kept in water that is too hard, fish and fry can suffer kidney damage.

When you see the cardinal and neon tetras close together, the difference in the body marking is clear. Adult cardinals are also a bit longer, at 2 in (5 cm), compared with the neons at 1.6 in (4 cm). Nothing matches the sight of a large shoal of neons darting through dense plant cover; they appear lit from within. For more information on neon tetras, including how to breed them, see pages 132-133.

NEON TETRA • *Paracheirodon innesi*

The neon tetra is probably the most popular of all aquarium fish. Today, nearly all the neons offered for sale are captive-bred, and some shops offer a choice of size: youngsters at 0.4-0.6 in (1-1.5 cm) and adult fish at 1.2-1.6 in (3-4 cm). Neons are a long-lived species; a 10-year lifespan is not uncommon.

A planted tank with an open area in the middle will display the fish at their best. Some people keep a tank just for neons and use a dark substrate, such as black gravel, and plenty of plants to create a stunning display. Although these tank-raised fish will tolerate a wide range of water parameters, they will not tolerate poor water management, which results in low oxygen levels and high nitrate levels.

Mature males are slimmer than females and have a straighter blue line along the flanks.

Ideal conditions

Water: Slightly acidic to neutral, soft to slightly hard.
Temperature: 68-79°F (20-26°C).
Food: Tiny live or frozen aquatic invertebrates, such as daphnia, mosquito larvae, and bloodworm. Flake foods. Provide a varied diet to maintain the colors of the fish.
Minimum number in the aquarium: A shoal of at least 6 and preferably 10 fish, because they really are at their best when seen in numbers.
Minimum tank size: 24 in (60 cm).
Tank region: Middle.

Size: *Males and females 1.6 in (4 cm)*

▶ Origins

The River Putumayo in Peru.

Safety first

House this gentle little fish with like companions and avoid keeping it with larger species, such as angels, because these will eat small neons.

▶ Breeding

Breeding takes place in very soft acidic water and subdued lighting. The eggs are laid over fine-leaved plants and hatch in 24 hours. Feed the newly hatched fry on very fine live foods.

Rearing the fry

Feed infusoria or a liquid fry food for the first week to 10 days, after which the fry will be able to take newly hatched brine shrimp. They are greedy feeders, and it is possible for them to gorge themselves to the point where serious internal damage occurs. They grow quickly, but are over 0.4 in (1 cm) long before they color up. Asian-bred and wild-caught fish tend to produce small numbers of healthy fry, but once these have been reared up by the breeder, second generation broods can number up to 400 healthy young.

Breeding setup

Tank measuring 24x12x12 in (60x30x30 cm).

Paint or cover the back and sides with black, and position the tank away from direct light.

Water temperature 77°F (25°C). Very soft water at pH 6 or lower.

Provide Java moss as a spawning medium.

Waterlogged peat substrate.

SPLASH TETRA • *Copella arnoldi*

These slightly larger characins for the community aquarium are active fish that like to be kept in shoals or at least pairs. It is difficult to distinguish between the sexes in young fish, so you would have to buy at least two! Keep them in an aquarium with a good cover glass, because they jump. They also like to feed from the surface and often flip from the water when doing so. A couple of floating plants will help deter jumping by giving the fish a secluded place to lurk in. Keep water conditions within bounds, ensuring that regular water changes and efficient filtration prevent any buildup of nitrates.

These fish will eat just about anything, from flies and flake floating on the surface to tablets that sink to the substrate. They also relish the usual range of live or frozen food.

▶ *Ideal conditions*

Water: Slightly acidic to neutral, soft to slightly hard.
Temperature: 73-84°F (23-29°C).
Food: Small live or frozen aquatic invertebrates, such as daphnia, mosquito larvae, and bloodworm. Flake foods.
Minimum number in the aquarium: 2.
Minimum tank size: 36 in (90 cm).
Tank region: Middle to top.

Mature males are generally larger and more colorful than females and have more extended finnage.

Size: Males 3.2 in (8 cm), females 2.4 in (6 cm)

▶ Breeding

Splash, or jumping, tetras are so called because of their method of spawning. To breed them, set up a special aquarium with a tight-fitting cover glass, because, with their bodies pressed together, a pair will jump and lay their eggs on the underside of a leaf overhanging the water surface at the top of the tank. The pair then fall back into the water and repeat the process until some 150 eggs have been laid. The male guards the eggs, flicking water at them to keep them moist until they hatch and the fry fall into the water. Provide them with tiny live foods.

▶ Origins

Guyana, lower Amazon.

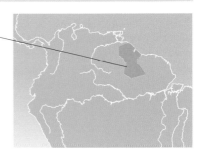

RED-EYED TETRA

MOENKHAUSIA SANCTAEFILOMENAE

The upper half of this fish's eye is bright red, hence the common name. It has a distinctive black band across the tail and dark-edged scales that give it an almost armor-plated appearance. These lovely shoaling fish from Brazil, Bolivia and Peru will swim toward the surface as well as in midwater and enjoy the cover provided in a well-planted aquarium. Choose plants carefully – these fish will damage soft-leaved varieties. Being slightly bigger than most tetras – adult size 2.75 in (7 cm) – they are best suited to a larger aquarium if you plan to keep a shoal.

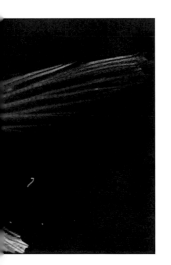

SERPAE TETRA • *Hyphessobrycon eques*

The serpae tetra is a deservedly popular fish due to its active behavior, character, and hardy nature. The color of the serpae tetra can vary depending on the breeding stock but is always a variation on a red-copper or rosy red color with a dark spot on the dorsal fin. Like most tetras, these fish will only do well when kept in groups, where they will shoal together. Occasional display fights are not uncommon but are simply a way for the fish to establish a natural hierarchy. The serpae tetra has a reputation for taking an occasional nip at a tankmate's fins, so avoid keeping these fish with any long-finned species. Coming from slow-moving waterways, the serpae tetra is accustomed to plenty of hiding spots among plants and roots, and should be provided with the same in the aquarium.

Breeding

Will breed fairly easily in soft acidic water in aquariums with densely planted areas, although the eggs are usually eaten in a community. The scattering of brownish eggs follows chasing and circling. The newly hatched larvae are particularly small, so feed them on infusoria or egg yolk.

The black spot on the dorsal fin adds variety to the aquarium as the fish dart around.

The serpae tetra brings constant movement to the display.

Ideal conditions

Water: Soft to medium, neutral to acidic.
Temperature: 72-79°F (22-26°C).
Food: Flake or dried foods, smaller frozen or live foods.
Minimum number in the aquarium: 5.
Minimum tank size: 24 in (60 cm).
Tank region: If tall plants are present, the fish will stay in the upper regions, otherwise lower to middle.

▶ Origins

Slow moving rivers and streams. Paraguay to Mato Grosso, Brazil.

The swimbladder shines through the rich, coppery body.

PENGUIN TETRA

THAYERIA BOEHLKEI

The dark "hockey stick" stripe along the center and lower caudal fin gives this fish a bold distinctive presence in the aquarium. It grows to 2.4 in (6 cm). The penguin tetra gets its name both from its markings and unusual movements. The fish often swims with its head slightly up and has a rather eye-catching jerky rocking motion. The penguin tetra is peaceful and will live in a wide range of water conditions. Females are slightly deeper-bodied than males and become very rounded when carrying eggs, of which there can be up to 1000!

GOLDEN PENCILFISH • *Nannostomus beckfordi*

Of all the pencilfish, this species is the easiest to keep. It will settle down well in a community aquarium with other small fishes but can be intimidated by larger, more boisterous ones. Avoid extremes of pH and hardness and ensure that the filtration is working well, because the fish do not like water with a lot of suspended matter in it. Provide some sheltered areas in the form of thickets of fine-leaved plants, such as cabomba.

Pencilfish can change their color pattern. During the day you can see the prominent longitudinal stripes. At night or in very dim conditions, these stripes break up until only vertical bars are visible on the body. This is nothing to worry about; it is perfectly normal.

Below: Having been well fed on plenty of live foods, this full-bodied female appears almost ready to spawn.

Ideal conditions

Water: Slightly acidic to neutral, soft to slightly hard.
Temperature: 73-79°F (23-26°C).
Food: Tiny live or frozen aquatic invertebrates, such as daphnia, mosquito larvae, and bloodworm that will fit into the fishes' small mouths. Regular feeds of live food maintain good coloration. Flake foods.
Minimum number in the aquarium: 2.
Minimum tank size: 24 in (60 cm).
Tank region: Middle.

▶ Origins

Guyana and in the lower River Negro, in the central Amazon region of Brazil.

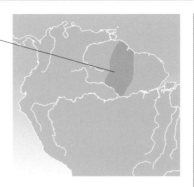

Males are slimmer than females and have white tips to their fins.

THREE-LINED PENCILFISH

NANNOSTOMUS TRIFASCIATUS

Pencilfish are a timid group that bring a sense of calm to the aquarium. Three-lined pencilfish have a wonderful set of markings based around three predominant horizontal stripes. Between the top two lines the body is gold and at the base of

each fin there is a scarlet red patch. In common with other pencilfishes, these bold stripes are replaced during the night by broad bars. Feed these midwater swimmers with flake food and provide them with some hiding places. Do not keep pencilfish with busy tankmates that will intimidate them. This midwater swimmer is found in the same area of Guyana and Brazil as the golden pencilfish. It spends most of its time holding station amid the security of plants, making it easy to take a long look at this charming little fish that grows to 4 in (10 cm).

SAILFIN MOLLY ● *Poecilia velifera*

These magnificent fish are very popular but can be difficult to keep properly. They need the correct diet, sufficient space, and only a gentle flow of water. They also require warmth and good-quality water; the hybrids in particular are susceptible to disease if conditions are not right. In nature, sailfin mollies regularly move between fresh and full-strength seawater. In captivity, the more salt in the water, the fewer disease problems they have. Wait until the aquarium has been established for six months or so to ensure stable conditions before you add these fish and then they should thrive.

The male uses his very large dorsal fin to display to females, and the anal fin is modified into a gonopodium. In some of the larger sailfin types, this may not develop until the fish is one year old or more. In the so-called green sailfin molly, the male's light olive-colored body looks silvery in bright light. Females are similarly colored but have a much smaller dorsal fin and no gonopodium. In some males, the dorsal fin may have a golden-orange edge, and the same color appears on the head and throat.

Breeding

The fish reach maturity in about nine months. A full-grown female may produce broods of up to 100 fry every month. The fry are large, up to 0.28 in (7 mm) in length when born. Given small live foods and plenty of algae to pick on, they grow rapidly.

Right: *A pair of sailfin mollies patrol the open water of the aquarium. The male shown here has an orange head and throat, whereas the female is basically silver with broken yellow stripes along the flanks. The male uses his impressive dorsal fin to display to the female.*

Size: Males 3.2 in (8 cm), females 3.5-4 in (9-10 cm)

▶ Origins

Southeastern
North Carolina
to the Atlantic
coast of Mexico.

▶ *Ideal conditions*

Water: Neutral, hard.
Temperature: 77-82°F (25-28°C).
Food: Small live or frozen aquatic invertebrates, such as daphnia, mosquito larvae, and bloodworm. Plenty of green foods. Flake foods.
Minimum number in the aquarium: One pair.
Minimum tank size: 36 in (90 cm).
Tank region: Middle to top.

The upturned mouth makes it easy for mollies to take food floating on the water surface.

SILVER SAILFIN MOLLY
POECILIA SPP.

This hybrid between the two most common molly species shows a lyre tail and a moderately tall dorsal fin. It grows to 7 in (18 cm). The more extreme silver balloon molly has a deep, foreshortened body.

ORANGE SAILFIN MOLLY
POECILIA VELIFERA

This is a farm-bred albino version of the green sailfin molly and lacks all the dark pigment. The sailfin characteristics are exaggerated in this fish, which grows to 7 in (18 cm). Note the gonopodium in the male shown below.

GUPPY or MILLIONS FISH • *Poecilia reticulata*

The guppy is one of the most popular aquarium fishes. It is bred commercially by the thousands and has been selectively bred to develop all the different colors and fin forms available today. These cultivated forms require higher temperatures than their wild counterparts. (Wild guppies are quite plain in comparison, but because they are rarely available, they are much sought after by dedicated hobbyists.) When buying your fish, be sure to include males and females. The males are the favorites because of their long, flowing caudal fins, and often gaudy colors. Although the females are less colorful – only their tails and sometimes the rear half of the body showing any color – the males do require something to show off to. Guppies have been introduced in some tropical regions to control mosquitoes, as they love eating the larvae.

Breeding

Male guppies are sexually mature at three months and the females earlier than that. They breed readily and a good-sized female may produce 20-40 young. Feed the fry on crumbled flake food or tiny frozen and live foods. To reduce the risk of larger tank mates eating the young, add floating plants.

This female has a colorful tail (but not as large as the male's) and a normal anal fin.

Ideal conditions

Water: Neutral, hard.
Temperature: 64-82°F (18-28°C).
Food: Small live or frozen aquatic invertebrates, such as daphnia, mosquito larvae, and bloodworm. Flake foods.
Minimum number in the aquarium: One pair.
Minimum tank size: 18 in (45 cm).
Tank region: Mid to top.

Size: *Males and females 2.4 in (6 cm)*

▶ Origins

Trinidad and
the adjacent
mainland of
Venezuela.

*This male king
cobra guppy has
a distinctively
banded tail.*

*As in other livebearers,
males have a
gonopodium – a modified
anal fin with which they
impregnate the female.*

Compatibility

Take care with
companions. The
flowing finnage of
the male guppies is
tempting as a snack to
other fish. Angels and
tiger barbs are
notorious for nipping
the trailing fins, and
the damage they cause
leaves open wounds
that are susceptible
to fungal attack.

NEON BLUE GUPPY
POECILIA RETICULATA

*The various guppy strains available in the
hobby, bearing names such as neon blue
(shown below), snakeskin, green lace,
golden, king cobra, half-black, or disco, may
breed true if they are kept apart. But most
hobbyists are content with a mixture,
waiting to see how the young turn out.*

GOLDEN GUPPY
POECILIA RETICULATA

*Avoid keeping the golden guppy with male
Siamese fighters of the same coloration,
which may mistake them for rivals and
attack them. Unlike their drab wild
ancestors, farmed guppies are available in
almost limitless permutations of coloration
and fin shape. Males are more flamboyant.*

*The orange and yellow
tail glistens in the
aquarium
lights.*

143

SWORDTAIL • *Xiphophorus helleri*

Swordtails are one of the mainstays of the aquarium trade. They have been bred to develop new colors and fin forms, but the red swordtail is still very popular. In good-quality fish, the color is a rich blood-red and the male will not develop his sword until he is quite large. Avoid small fish that are already showing their swords, as these will not mature into good specimens to breed from. You will still be able to sex them by checking for the gonopodium in the male. (Confusingly, females that have undergone a superficial sex change also develop a gonopodium.) Many color forms are available, including red, black, green, half-black, wagtail (red with a black tail), albino, and lyretail.

These active fish need plenty of swimming space, so confine the planting to the rear and sides of the aquarium. The fry also need sufficient room to grow, so avoid overcrowding them. They will feed by picking on algae and eating crumbled flake food.

Ideal conditions

Water: Neutral, slightly hard.
Temperature: 70-82°F (21-28°C).
Food: Small live or frozen aquatic invertebrates, such as daphnia, mosquito larvae, and bloodworm. Green foods. Flake foods.
Minimum number in the aquarium: One pair.
Minimum tank size: 36 in (90 cm).
Tank region: Mid to upper.

Breeding

Swordtails breed readily and can produce broods of as many as 80 young, many of which will survive in the community aquarium provided there are some fine-leaved plants or floating plants for cover and no fish large enough to eat them!

Female pineapple swordtail

Mature males exhibit a good sword.

Size: Males 4 in (10 cm), females 4.7 in (12 cm)

▶ Origins

Atlantic slope rivers in Southeast Mexico, Belize, and Guatemala.

Apparent sex change
Female swordtails occasionally take on male characteristics, i.e., develop a short "sword" on the tail.

RED WAG SWORDTAIL
XIPHOPHORUS HELLERI
The swordtail has been developed from its original green form into many color strains and with exaggerated fin forms. This striking form has a jet-black tail and sword.

Left: Be sure to buy swordtails of the same color forms as pairs, otherwise you will end up with some strange-looking crossbreeds in peculiar colors.

BLACK SWORDTAIL
XIPHOPHORUS HELLERI
This is the swordtail version of the closely related tuxedo platy, and interbreeding of the two species is suspected. In all male swordtails, the lower rays of the caudal fin are extended, hence the common name. Apparently stunted swordtail males are often the most fertile.

Male pineapple swordtail

PLATY • *Xiphophorus maculatus*

The platy is an excellent fish for the novice aquarist. It adapts well to aquarium life and makes a welcome, colorful addition to the community tank. The fish are peaceful, even with each other. Males can be distinguished from females by their gonopodium and, in mature fish, smaller size. They like to nibble at plants if insufficient green foods are offered but do little damage, usually only taking algae from the leaves. Plant the tank with more robust plants, such as vallisneria, Amazon swordplants, and Java fern.

Like its near relative, the swordtail, it has been developed to produce such well-known forms as red, wagtail, moon, tuxedo, blue hifin, and sunset, to name but a few!

Ideal conditions

Water: Neutral, slightly hard.
Temperature: 70-77°F (21-25°C).
Food: Small live or frozen aquatic invertebrates, such as daphnia, mosquito larvae, and bloodworm. Green foods. Flake foods.
Minimum number in the aquarium: One pair.
Minimum tank size: 18 in (45 cm).
Tank region: Mid to upper.

Above: *Adult platies, being less than half the size of adult swordtails, make good community fish for those aquarists who only have space for a small aquarium. This is a male.*

Red wagtail platies should have a blood-red body and jet black fins.

Size: Males 1.2 in (3 cm), females 2.5 in (6 cm)

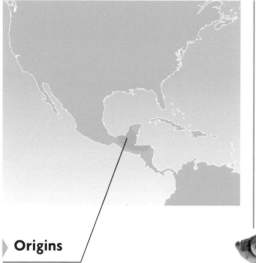

▸ Origins

Mexico, Guatemala,
and Northern
Honduras.

▸ Breeding

Platies will breed readily and
even in the confines of the
community tank, the young
can reach maturity. They are
mature at about four months
old and, fortunately, do not
produce large broods. They
therefore are much easier for
the novice to cope with than
the more prolific swordtail.

TUXEDO PLATY

XIPHOPHORUS MACULATUS

*In their smart but understated formal livery, tuxedo
platies are a good foil to examples with more showy
coloration. Be aware that all strains readily
interbreed, so try to keep them separate. The fish
shown below is a female. In platies, the sexes are
easily told apart by the anal fin; in the male, it has
become modified into an internal organ of
fertilization known as a gonopodium (see also
Breeding pages 64–65).*

Left: These are
color forms of
variatus platies
(X. variatus). The
two males at the
top are hifin
types, with a
larger dorsal fin
than normal
forms. The two
females below
are sunset forms.

SIAMESE FIGHTING FISH • *Betta splendens*

The highly colored fish that are offered for sale today have been captive bred to produce a wide variety of colors and extended finnage. The male is the flamboyant one with the long fins, while the females are fairly dowdy with short fins.

Siamese fighting fish need warmth; aim to maintain a stable temperature, as fluctuations can cause stress and leave the fish open to infection. The other major cause of injury is keeping fighting fish with unsuitable companions that nip their trailing finnage. The damaged fins are then susceptible to fungal and bacterial attack.

Provide an aquarium with plants that not only reach the surface but also grow in thickets that will provide a refuge for these beautiful fish.

Healthy, happy fighters such as this one display their finnage to its best advantage.

Ideal conditions

Water: Neutral, to slightly hard.
Temperature: 75-86°F (24-30°C).
Food: Small live or frozen aquatic invertebrates, such as daphnia, mosquito larvae, and bloodworm. Flake foods.
Minimum number in the aquarium: Single male.
Minimum tank size: 18 in (45 cm).
Tank region: Top.

Size: Males and females 2.4-2.7 in (6-7 cm)

Above: *A male steel-blue Siamese fighter shows off his beautiful trailing finnage, which is far more elaborate than in the wild fish. Avoid fin-nipping tank mates.*

▶ **Origins**

Thailand and Cambodia.

Above: *Devoted parent but merciless to other males, the male Siamese fighter lives its short life on the edge. Flowing fins and flared gill covers are displayed as threat gestures that quickly develop into ferocious attacks on each other's fins. A sole male will live peacefully in a community aquarium, but a breeding pair need a well-planted tank to themselves.*

Compatibility

You can keep a single male in one tank (other inmates permitting!) or even a male and several females but do not keep two males together. These fish were originally bred for their belligerence and two males will fight, often to the death. The initial threat postures of spread gill covers and flared fins quickly develop into a series of attacks when the fish rip each other's fins.

DWARF GOURAMI • *Colisa lalia*

These small gouramis are ideal for a peaceful community aquarium, but do not be tempted to add them to a new tank; wait a few months until things have settled down and stabilized before you contemplate buying them. Wild-caught fish are harder to acclimatize than their tank-bred counterparts. Fortunately, those offered for sale are tank raised, so will settle better in your display aquarium.

Buy a pair; in fact, they are usually sold this way. It is easy to tell the males from the females by their color: females are more silvery, whereas males have red and blue bars along their bodies. Several color forms are also available.

In this aquarium strain, blue is the dominant coloration, although you can still see the flank bars showing through. This is a male fish.

Ideal conditions

Water: Neutral, soft to slightly hard.
Temperature: 72-82°F (22-28°C).
Food: Small live or frozen aquatic invertebrates, such as daphnia, mosquito larvae, and bloodworm. Flake foods.
Minimum number in the aquarium: One pair.
Minimum tank size: 18 in (45 cm).
Tank region: Middle to top.

The female is more silvery than the male. When she is ready to spawn, the stomach becomes distended.

150

Size: Males and females 2 in (5 cm)

▶ **Origins**

*India: Ganges,
Brahmaputra,
Jumna drainages.*

Health alert

*Pay particular attention to
water quality; if you forget a
water change, the fish could
be in trouble. If conditions do
deteriorate, the fins may
become ragged, the fish may
go off their food and sulk in a
quiet part of the tank. At
worst, they may develop a
bacterial infection.*

ROYAL RED GOURAMI
COLISA LALIA

*In the royal red gourami, only the more pointed dorsal
fin of the male is a sure way of identifying the sexes.
The humped shoulder profile is typical of dwarf gouramis.
They are peaceable, if somewhat shy.*

*Fish that live in oxygen-deficient waters must swim to
the surface to avoid suffocation. The anabantids have
developed an accessory breathing organ to cope with
conditions in which the gills alone would be unable to
supply enough oxygen for their needs (see also page 155).*

Female

*Male royal red
gourami*

PEARL GOURAMI • *Trichogaster leeri*

These beautiful fish are best kept in a larger community aquarium where they can swim and display to each other. Males have more intense colors and longer finnage than the females. It is safe to keep more than one male, provided there is plenty of plant cover in the tank. The males may spar with each other but rarely do any real damage.

The pearl gourami is a hardy, long-lived species and an ideal fish for the novice aquarist. However, do not let the water temperature drop below the minimum given below. If the fish become chilled, at best they often go off their food and sulk, at worst they fall ill.

Compatibility

Choose companion species with care. Avoid any that may bully the gourami – cichlids are especially noted for their aggressive tendencies. In such situations, the gouramis refuse to eat, sulk in a corner, and lose their color.

▶ *Ideal conditions*

Water: Neutral, soft to slightly hard.
Temperature: 75-82°F (24-28°C).
Food: They relish small live or frozen aquatic invertebrates, such as daphnia, mosquito larvae, and bloodworm. Flake and green foods.
Minimum number in the aquarium: One pair.
Minimum tank size: 36 in (90 cm).
Tank region: Middle to top.

Size: Males and females 4 in (10 cm)

Breeding bubble-nesters

Gouramis build nests of bubbles at the surface, often incorporating pieces of plant to give them more stability. However, some species build a nest under a plant leaf or in a cave. The larger gourami species (pearls, moonlights, golds, and blues) can produce huge broods of young; broods of more than 2000 have been known and clearly, most hobbyists cannot hope to rear them all. If you try, they will be stunted and may end up polluting their water to the point where most are poisoned by their own wastes.

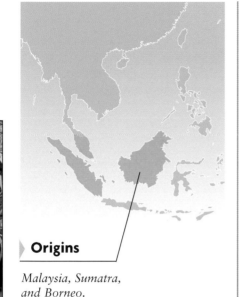

▶ **Origins**

Malaysia, Sumatra, and Borneo.

The flowing fins are a great temptation to fin-nipping species, and damaged fins can be affected by fungus.

▶ *Breeding*

When breeding, the pair will build a bubble nest for the eggs and subsequent fry.

Tank measuring 24x12x12 in (60x30x30 cm).

Water hardness and pH are not critical, as this fish will adapt to a wide range of conditions.

75-80°F (24-27°C).

Caves for females to hide in if harassed.

Floating plants such as Riccia fluitans.

BLUE GOURAMI • *Trichogaster trichopterus*

Because it is easy to keep and breed, this is a favorite fish among novice aquarists. The blue, or three-spot, gourami is one of the mainstays of the aquarium trade. It is also available in a gold and opaline form (shown here). The fish are omnivorous and will eat anything from flakes to flies.

Young fish are not always easy to sex, but, as they mature, the males develop a more pointed dorsal fin and their color is a little more intense. Males are very vigorous drivers at breeding time, so remove the female after spawning is complete.

Blue gouramis are very useful in the aquarium because of their willingness to eat planarian worms, which saves you having to add any chemicals to the aquarium to eliminate these pests.

Ideal conditions

Water: Neutral, soft to slightly hard.
Temperature: 72-82°F (22-28°C).
Food: Small live or frozen aquatic invertebrates, such as daphnia, mosquito larvae, and bloodworm. Flake foods.
Minimum number in the aquarium: One pair.
Minimum tank size: 36 in (90 cm).
Tank region: Middle to top.

This is the opaline form of the three-spot gourami.

Size: Males and females 4 in (10 cm)

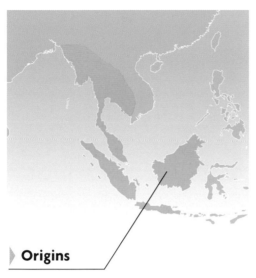

▶ Origins

Southeast Asia: Burma, Thailand, Malaysia, and Indonesia.

Compatibility

Although they are relatively peaceful with other fish, males can become aggressive toward each other, especially as they age. It may be necessary to move one male to another aquarium if they are damaging each other. Despite this, they are well worth keeping, but make sure they are not bullied by companion species.

Air breathing

Many fish have developed a method of taking in bubbles of air to survive, but in pools that are prone to periodic drying up or that become stagnant and foul because of dead and rotting vegetation, the ability to take in air at the water surface is crucial to the fish's survival. The anabantids' labyrinth-like accessory breathing organ is made up of outgrowths from the pharynx or the branchial (gill) chamber. These are filled with a spongy structure that has a large surface area richly supplied with blood vessels. Oxygen diffuses into these vessels from air stored in the labyrinth organ.

Accessory breathing organ

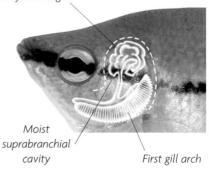

Highly branched labyrinth organ

Moist suprabranchial cavity

First gill arch

It is from the labyrinth organ that anabantids have acquired their common name, the labyrinth fish.

KISSING GOURAMI • *Helostoma temmincki*

This species is often kept just for the novelty of seeing the fish "kiss." However, the act has nothing to do with passion, but more with trials of strength to determine pecking order within a shoal or territorial boundaries. Despite this, they are a peaceable species that rarely do each other physical damage. These gouramis have normal pelvic fins, and the sexes are virtually impossible to distinguish.

Although the fish relish algae, you will need to feed them other foods, too. Offer flakes, frozen and also green foods. If you accustom them to eating frozen peas and some lettuce leaves, they will choose these in preference to your prized plants. To gain extra nourishment, these fish are also capable of filtering plankton through their gills.

To see them at their best, provide a spacious aquarium decorated with rocks, wood, and broadleaved plants. Keep the water clean and well filtered.

Above: The green morph is less frequently available than the pink, but well worth keeping for its more subtle coloration.

Iridescent pink is the most widely seen coloration in the aquarium trade.

Since it is impossible to tell the sexes apart, these are just as likely to be two sparring males or females as a true pair.

In the wild, the kissing gourami is found in the poorly oxygenated waters of sluggish streams, swamps and pools.

Size: Males and females 6-12 in (15-30 cm)

Origins

The green form is found
in Burma, Thailand,
Malaysia, and Indonesia.
The pink form was first
developed in Java.

Ideal conditions

Water: Neutral, soft to slightly hard.
Temperature: 72-82°F (22-28°C).
Food: Small, live or frozen aquatic
invertebrates, such as daphnia,
mosquito larvae, and bloodworm.
Green foods and flake foods.
Minimum number in the aquarium: 1.
Minimum tank size: 36 in (90 cm).
Tank region: Middle to top.

HONEY GOURAMI
COLISA SOTA

*Being one of the smaller gourami species – maximum adult
size 2 in (5 cm) – the honey gourami from India, Assam, and
Bangladesh is ideally suited to the smaller setup. The
glorious honey color is seen in the male, which also has
a dark blue-black head and belly. To thrive, the honey
gourami prefers dense plant cover in which to hide. Like
all gouramis, these fish can become territorial when they
breed, so the plant cover helps to protect both them and
other fish in the aquarium. Keep with peaceful species only.*

Algae eaters

*In the aquarium, one of their greatest assets is the control of
algae, especially in a new aquarium. It does not matter whether
you buy the pink or the green form; a couple of youngsters
added to a new setup will happily go around the tank browsing
on the algae. Although they eat vegetation, youngsters tend to
eat the algae in preference to the plants, making them both
useful and decorative. Their drawback is that they become
quite large and may outgrow your aquarium.*

BRONZE CORYDORAS • *Corydoras aeneus*

Corydoras aeneus is ideal for the novice fishkeeper. It is easy to feed and like all the *Corydoras* species, but unlike some other catfish, active during the day. The fish dig into the substrate for food, so keep them in an aquarium with a fine, rounded substrate, such as river sand or fine gravel, otherwise they could damage their delicate barbels. Although they dig, they do not uproot your plants. If you watch them carefully, they are sifting through the substrate as they would in the wild to find small worms and other tiny invertebrates. This hardy species will flourish in the aquarium temperature range recommended but can tolerate temperatures as low as 50°F (10°C) for brief periods.

Being a widespread species, the color on *C. aeneus* can vary. It can also vary because the majority of the fish now available are captive bred on fish farms. An albino form is also available.

Ideal conditions

Water: Slightly acidic to slightly alkaline, slightly soft to slightly hard.
Temperature: 72-79°F (22-26°C).
Food: Small live or frozen aquatic invertebrates, such as daphnia, mosquito larvae, and bloodworm. Flake, tablet, and granular food.
Minimum number in the aquarium: 2.
Minimum tank size: 24 in (60 cm).
Tank region: Bottom.

Compatibility

All Corydoras *species are shoaling fish that will happily shoal with other* Corydoras *species, so you need not keep them in single species groups.*

Members of this family have two rows of bony plates along their sides.

A varied diet that includes live or frozen foods helps to maintain the subtle greenish-bronze hues.

Size: *Males and females 3.5 in (9 cm)*

▶ Origins

Coastal rivers of Southeast Brazil and Uruguay.

▶ *Breeding*

The female holds two or three eggs in her cupped pelvic fins while they are fertilized and then presses them onto a leaf. The fry grow rapidly if fed on newly hatched brine shrimp.

This color strain adds zest to the display.

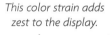

ALBINO BRONZE CORY
CORYDORAS AENEUS
Albino corydoras catfish were originally spontaneous mutations lacking black pigment but are now bred to order. They grow to a mature size of 2.75 in (7 cm).

SUNSET CORY
CORYDORAS SP.
Feeding to improve natural coloration may have an influence on these startlingly bright corydoras catfish, and this is a perfectly acceptable practice. Not so is the injection of dye into mass-farmed tropical fish, though it still goes on, particularly with Indian glassfish. If you suspect your aquatic shop knowingly stocks dyed fish, take your business elsewhere. Nature's diversity should not be abused in this way.

STERBA'S CORYDORAS • *Corydoras sterbai*

The *Corydoras* group of catfish have been a popular addition to community aquariums for a long time and now there are more varieties than ever. One that stands out of the "new crowd" is Sterba's corydoras. The complex patterning of this striped and mottled fish make it an attractive addition to any aquarium. All corydoras need to be kept in groups, and although they often spend time foraging alone, when at rest, they will almost always take up position next to another of the same species. Their sensitive barbels help them search the substrate for food. In the aquarium, they appreciate a few patches of dense vegetation along with open areas in which to scavenge.

Ideal conditions

Water: Soft to medium, neutral to acidic.
Temperature: 68-79°F (20-26°C).
Food: Sinking foods, regular frozen or live foods such as bloodworm.
Minimum number in the aquarium: 3.
Minimum tank size: 24 in (60 cm).
Tank region: Bottom.

Ripe females become quite rotund compared with males.

Breeding

Females are more rounded than males. Small clutches of adhesive eggs are laid on leaves or other flat surfaces, and these hatch in 4-5 days. The young can be fed on daphnia or brine shrimp.

Right: With space and good food, the young Sterba's cory at the top could reach breeding size within about six to eight months.

Size: *Males and females 3.2 in (8 cm)*

▶ **Origins**

Rio Guapore, Brazil

Ideal water

C. gossei *prefers slightly acid water. Your dealer should have fish acclimatized to the local water conditions.*

GOSSE'S CORYDORAS
CORYDORAS GOSSEI

Comparing the pastel colors of Corydoras gossei *with the mottling of* C. sterbai *illustrates the differences of patterning within the corydoras group. In* C. gossei, *the dark body with lighter underside and yellow finnage makes for a more subtle fish that looks particularly good against the dark sandy substrate that these fish prefer. The large number of corydoras varieties is accounted for by their distribution over virtually all of the South American tributaries that feed into the Amazon Basin. Almost every tributary has its own species of corydoras:* C. gossei, *measuring 2 in (5 cm), comes from the Mamore River in Bolivia.*

In the aquarium, C. gossei *looks even better when kept together with a group of* C. sterbai.

Small rounded substrates or sand prevent damage to the delicate barbels.

PORTHOLE CATFISH or DIANEMA • *Dianema longibarbis*

Dianema are well suited to the larger community aquarium stocked with medium-sized, peaceful fishes. They like plenty of swimming space and some open areas of substrate on which to feed. Like corydoras, to which they are related, they feed by sifting through the substrate. Make sure this is fine, with well-rounded grains, so that the fishes' delicate barbels and even their eyes are not damaged if they delve too deeply.

When buying your fish, look to see that they are active and that their fins, especially the caudal, are held out well. The first signs of their displeasure at deteriorating or inappropriate tank conditions are clamped fins, followed by degeneration of the barbels. Avoid fish showing these symptoms.

Dianema eat most small foods, be they live, frozen, or dried. They usually prefer feeding at dusk and dawn, so drop some tablet food into the tank just before you turn out the lights.

Ideal conditions

Water: Slightly acidic to slightly alkaline, slightly soft to slightly hard.
Temperature: 72-79°F (22-26°C).
Food: Small live or frozen aquatic invertebrates, such as daphnia, mosquito larvae, and bloodworm. Flake, tablet, and sinking granules.
Minimum number in the aquarium: 2.
Minimum tank size: 36 in (90 cm).
Tank region: Bottom to middle.

Breeding

This fish is rarely bred. It builds a bubble nest, and the male, the slimmer of the pair, guards the eggs and fry.

Healthy fish show good color and finnage.

Size: Males and females 3.5 in (9 cm)

▶ Origins

The Peruvian Amazon.

EMERALD CATFISH
BROCHIS SPLENDENS
The longer dorsal fin is an instant clue, showing that these callichthyids, found in rivers in Peru, Ecuador, and Brazil, are not true Corydoras, although they are very closely related. Growing to 2.75 in (7 cm), brochis are more robustly built, deeper in the body, with a more massive head and a longer snout, but in temperament there are no real differences between the genera. They lay large, adhesive eggs on flat vertical or horizontal surfaces.

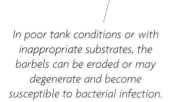

In poor tank conditions or with inappropriate substrates, the barbels can be eroded or may degenerate and become susceptible to bacterial infection.

Above: *Brochis catfish are more active when kept in groups of between four and six specimens. They prefer a deep aquarium.*

ZEBRA CATFISH • *Hypancistrus zebra*

It is not hard to see why this fish is always in high demand; it is one of the most stunningly patterned suckermouth catfishes seen in the hobby. In the wild, these fish are found in sunlit shallow waterways with a gravelly bottom. When viewed from above in this environment, they are surprisingly hard to see. The zebra catfish is an ideal aquarium fish for medium-soft water. It will not grow as large as some suckermouth catfishes and is a good algae eater. Being nocturnal, it will hide under pieces of wood or decor during the day and come out in the evening and at night to graze algae.

▶ *Ideal conditions*

Water: Acidic to neutral, soft to medium hard.
Temperature: 73-79°F (23-26°C).
Food: Vegetable-based sinking foods. Make sure it gets its fair share of the food on offer.
Minimum number in the aquarium: 1.
Minimum tank size: 24 in (60 cm).
Tank region: Bottom.

The distinct patterning of these fish has earned them another common name – "Humbug catfish."

Availability

Price fluctuations have been a major issue, but, with a growing trend toward the captive breeding of these fish, it is hoped that they will be available to everyone at reasonable prices.

Size: Males and females 3.2 in (8 cm)

▶ Origins

Xingu River Basin,
South America

▶ *Breeding*

Eggs are laid in
clutches in a cavelike
area, and the male
tends the eggs while
both fish guard and
protect the area.

PIMELODUS CATFISH
PIMELODUS PICTUS

*The reflective silvery body of the pictus
catfish is shared by few fish in the hobby but
is especially noticeable in this one. Other
features include the distinctive markings,
long whiskers, and constant activity. The fin
rays have sharp serrations that can cause
injury, so handle it with care. Never try to
catch these fish with a net, as they become
entangled and impossible to remove. Instead,
use a bag or solid container. The pictus
catfish grows to 6 in (15 cm) and will routinely
eat fish up to 2 in (5 cm) long. Not suitable
for a community aquarium.*

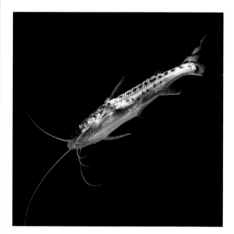

Above: *Seen against a black background,
the sleek silver body of the pictus catfish
makes a striking display. The barbels are
very long and slender.*

*Males have a
spinier leading edge
to the pectoral fins.*

BRISTLENOSE • *Ancistrus* spp.

There are several species of *Ancistrus* that all look very similar. In the aquarium, their behavior and needs are much the same. These little catfish will help to get rid of the algae that plagues every fishkeeper at some time, but it does not stop there. It will also eat the odd broad-leaved plant if you do not feed it extra green foods, such as lettuce, zucchini, and peas. Bristlenoses are constant grazers, and we cannot grow sufficient algae in an aquarium to satisfy them, hence the need for additional foods.

Provide the fish with areas of shelter for the daytime and open areas of substrate that they can grub over during the hours of darkness. They like clean, clear, well-oxygenated water and should the oxygen levels fall – for example, during extended hot weather – they will be found close to the water surface, where the oxygen levels are a little higher. A good external power filter with a spray bar return or additional aeration from an air pump will help alleviate such situations.

▶ *Ideal conditions*

Water: Slightly acidic to neutral, soft to slightly hard.
Temperature: 72-80°F (22-27°C).
Food: Green foods, plus small aquatic invertebrates, especially frozen bloodworm. May take flake and tablet foods.
Minimum number in the aquarium: One pair.
Minimum tank size: 36 in (90 cm).
Tank region: Bottom.

Males have large bushy bristles on and around the head; females just have a row of very fine bristles around the snout.

Size: *Males and females 4.7 in (12 cm)*

▶ Origins

Tropical South America.

Above: *This is the leucistic (semi-albino) form of the bristlenose catfish.*

Compatibility

Bristlenoses are territorial and will squabble with other bottom-dwelling fish, as well as with each other if you try to crowd them.

▶ Breeding

Ancistrus is the easiest of the suckermouths to spawn in an aquarium. The male broods a clutch of orange eggs under a rock or in a cave.

Above: *In the wild, the fish suck onto surfaces to avoid being swept away by water currents.*

167

OTOCINCLUS • *Otocinclus* sp.

This small catfish likes a well-planted aquarium and small, peaceful companions. Like other loricariids, it has stout fin spines and three rows of bony plates along its body for protection. Beware when handling the fish, as they may become entangled in the net. Do not attempt to pull a fish free; either let it free itself or carefully cut away the net.

Remember that this creature is for the most part herbivorous. It is one of the best algae eaters for the aquarium, but it is very rare for an aquarium to provide enough algae to satisfy its needs. You therefore must offer plenty of green foods in the diet. The easiest way is to supply frozen peas or "plant" lettuce leaves in the substrate for the fish to graze over. Be sure to remove old leaves and peas before they start to decompose.

Otocinclus are not happy if the water conditions begin to deteriorate. They go off their food and may hang near the surface. Regular water changes and efficient filtration should help avoid this situation.

Algae eaters

The popular algae-eating Otocinclus *species, of which* several *examples are available, are much better suited to a display than the traditional algae loach* (Gymnocheilus aymonieri), *which usually grows aggressive in the aquarium. The placid* Otocinclus *species, however, grazes the entire tank of all algae, other than blue-green and brush algae.*

▶ *Ideal conditions*

Water: Slightly acidic to slightly alkaline, slightly soft to slightly hard.
Temperature: 68-79°F (20-26°C).
Food: Flake and tablet food. Algae and green foods.
Minimum number in the aquarium: 2.
Minimum tank size: 18 in (45 cm).
Tank region: Bottom to middle.

Size: Males and females 1.6 in (4 cm)

▶ Origins

In fast-flowing streams near Rio de Janeiro, Brazil.

▶ Breeding

Otocinclus breed by laying their eggs on plant leaves. The eggs can take up to 72 hours to hatch. The fry require very fine live foods and green foods.

This is a typical resting position for an otocinclus. This young fish appears to be grasping the leaf with its pelvic fins.

BUTTERFLY PLEC
PECKOLTIA PULCHER

This is one little loricariid catfish that does not cause too much trouble in the community aquarium. For most of the day, it lurks beneath a stone or under plants, but in the evening it rummages around the aquarium in search of its favorite food – algae. Now, no matter how hard you try, the tank can never grow enough algae to keep it happy, so be sure to provide alternatives in the form of lettuce, frozen peas, zucchini, and potato. Despite being a herbivore, it leaves the plants alone, neither digging them up nor eating them. Little is known of its breeding habits.

P. pulcher requires clean water with a reasonable oxygen content. It makes no demands on its companions, as it tends to keep to itself. However it is inclined to be quarrelsome with its own kind, especially if there is not enough room for each one to have its own territory. Keep only one fish in a 24x12 in (60x30 cm) tank. In a 36 in (90 cm) tank, you could probably keep two.

ROYAL WHIPTAIL • *Sturisoma panamense*

The stunning royal whiptail is well worth keeping if you have a larger, well-established community aquarium with fish that will not pick at the catfish's trailing finnage. It is not suitable for a newly set up tank.

To keep the fish healthy, pay particular attention to maintaining water quality. It should be well filtered, with a high oxygen content. They will graze on green food, as well as taking commercially prepared foods that sink, and frozen and live bloodworm and daphnia – yes, even these bottom dwellers are partial to daphnia and are comical to watch while catching it!

Keep them in a tank with open areas of substrate for them to feed over. They will also rasp over wood and plants but, provided you give them enough alternative green foods, they do little, if any, damage to plants.

Ideal conditions

Water: Slightly acidic to slightly alkaline, slightly soft to slightly hard.
Temperature: 72-80°F (22-27°C).
Food: Small live or frozen aquatic invertebrates, such as daphnia, mosquito larvae, and bloodworm. Flake food. Algae and green foods.
Minimum number in the aquarium: One pair.
Minimum tank size: 36 in (90 cm).
Tank region: Bottom to middle.

Breeding

The fish will breed in captivity, often laying their eggs on the aquarium glass. The male guards and cleans the eggs. The fry require very tiny foods such as infusoria (tiny ciliate animals).

Males have cheek bristles during the breeding season and are generally slimmer than females when viewed from above.

Size: *Males and females 10 in (25 cm)*

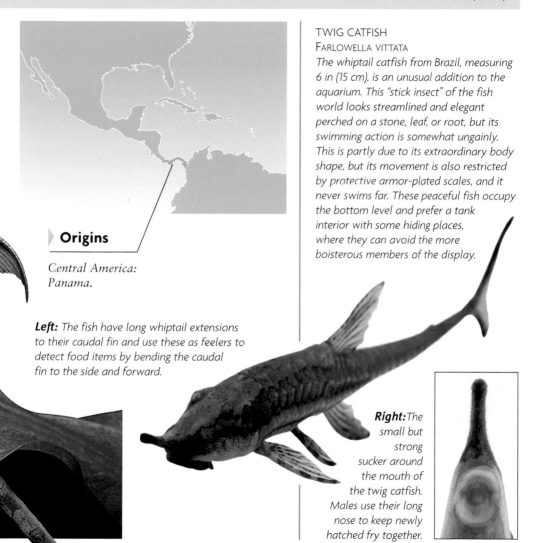

Origins

*Central America:
Panama.*

Left: *The fish have long whiptail extensions to their caudal fin and use these as feelers to detect food items by bending the caudal fin to the side and forward.*

TWIG CATFISH
FARLOWELLA VITTATA
The whiptail catfish from Brazil, measuring 6 in (15 cm), is an unusual addition to the aquarium. This "stick insect" of the fish world looks streamlined and elegant perched on a stone, leaf, or root, but its swimming action is somewhat ungainly. This is partly due to its extraordinary body shape, but its movement is also restricted by protective armor-plated scales, and it never swims far. These peaceful fish occupy the bottom level and prefer a tank interior with some hiding places, where they can avoid the more boisterous members of the display.

Right: *The small but strong sucker around the mouth of the twig catfish. Males use their long nose to keep newly hatched fry together.*

UPSIDE-DOWN CATFISH • *Synodontis nigriventris*

The upside-down catfish is always a talking point because of its way of swimming. In the wild, it is found beneath floating logs and vegetation, where it swims inverted, feeding on insects that land on the water surface and on prey items, such as mosquito larvae. Its coloration is suited to its lifestyle. The belly is dark brown so that passing predators, such as birds, cannot easily see it when they look into the water, while its back is a much lighter brown, so that when seen by predators in the water beneath it, it blends into the logs and plants debris. Most active at dawn and dusk, it can be tempted out at almost any time by food. It will take flake food from the surface and is not averse to turning up the right way and taking a pellet or tablet from the substrate! These peaceful creatures are quite at home in the community aquarium.

▶ *Ideal conditions*

Water: Slightly acidic to slightly alkaline, slightly soft to slightly hard.
Temperature: 72-79°F (22-26°C).
Food: Small live or frozen aquatic invertebrates, such as daphnia, mosquito larvae, and bloodworm. Flake food.
Minimum number in the aquarium: 6.
Minimum tank size: 24 in (60 cm).
Tank region: Middle to top.

In the aquarium, these fish feel secure with plants that reach to the surface and wood that arches over to provide a retreat.

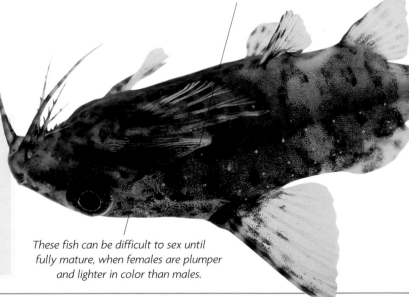

Branched barbels provide the fish with a large sensory area to seek food.

Health check

If there is a problem with the water, the barbels will begin to degenerate. If this happens, do a water change and check that the filtration system is working properly.

These fish can be difficult to sex until fully mature, when females are plumper and lighter in color than males.

Size: Males 3 in (7.5 cm), females 4 in (10 cm)

▶ Origins

Central Africa: Zaire Basin.

Breeding

House an individual pair in a well-planted 18 in (45 cm) aquarium and condition them on plenty of live foods. Since they may be seasonal spawners, it could be many months before they spawn.

Once settled into their new quarters, the pair will stake out a particular cave as their home. When they are in spawning condition, they dig a pit in the substrate and lay their eggs into it. Since the pit is normally dug under an overhang during the night, you may not realize right away that spawning has taken place. Both parents protect the nest and newly hatched young.

Set the temperature at 79°F (26°C).

Vallisneria

Small cryptocorynes

Tank measuring 24x12x12 in (60x30x30 cm).

Soft, slightly acidic water (pH 6.5).

▶ Breeding

These fish have been captive bred. Males are slimmer and smaller than females. The best natural food to bring them into spawning condition is mosquito larvae. The eggs are deposited in a depression in the substrate, and both parents care for the eggs and fry.

Arrange the rockwork and bogwood into several caves.

Sandy substrate

GLASS CATFISH • *Kryptopterus bicirrhis*

Catfish are often the last to be considered for a community aquarium, because it is mistakenly believed that they are scavengers and therefore not very interesting. Nothing could be further from the truth with the glass catfish. These midwater shoaling fish are active during the day, feeding in the same manner as tetras and barbs. And they have an added attraction: you can see right through them! The silvery sac at the front of the fish houses its delicate organs, while the transparent body allows you to view the spine and fin rays with ease. You can even see the plants behind them!

Despite their bizarre appearance, they are not too difficult to keep. Be sure to maintain the water quality and provide them with a reasonable flow of water through the tank (they like to swim in this). Keep a minimum of four fish; single specimens feel insecure, will hide away, refuse to eat, and may die. At rest, the fish hang at an angle, but, when swimming, they are horizontal.

Ideal conditions

Water: Slightly acidic to slightly alkaline, slightly soft to slightly hard.
Temperature: 70-79°F (21-26°C).
Food: Small live or frozen aquatic invertebrates, such as daphnia, mosquito larvae, and bloodworm. Flake food.
Minimum number in the aquarium: 4.
Minimum tank size: 24 in (60 cm).
Tank region: Middle to top.

When swimming, glass catfish are horizontal. At rest, they hang tail down, their bodies at an angle.

Size: Males and females 5 in (13 cm)

The swimbladder

In most of the bony fishes, the swimbladder acts as a hydrostatic organ, or float, that enables the fish to remain at any depth without rising or falling in the water column. To arrive at such a state, the density of the fish and that of the surrounding water must be just about equal. To achieve this in freshwater fish, the swimbladder (within the silvery sac shown below) needs to occupy 7-8% of the body volume.

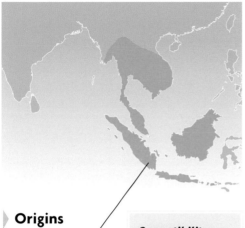

In most freshwater fish, the swimbladder has an open duct to the gut.

▶ Origins

Thailand, Malaysia, and Indonesia.

Compatibility

Keep these peaceful fish with tank mates of 1.6 in (4 cm) or more. Good-sized glass catfish may eat fry or even small neons.

▶ Breeding

Little is known of the breeding habits of glass catfish, although there are reports of accidental spawnings when fry have just appeared in the aquarium. The fry were then raised on infusoria followed by daphnia.

Usually located just below the vertebral column, the swimbladder forms a center of buoyancy, and its position can determine whether the fish adopts a head-down, head-up, or horizontal pose when at rest.

CHAIN LOACH or DWARF LOACH ● *Botia sidthimunki*

Chain, or dwarf, loaches are peaceful, active fish that are out and about during the day. Be sure to keep them as a group so that they can interact with each other. Although they are predominantly bottom-dwelling fish, you can often see them resting on the leaves of broad-leaved plants, such as Amazon swordplants. Provide a fine substrate so that they can dig for small items of food without causing any discernible damage to the decor! Before adding chain loaches to the tank, wait until the water has had time to mature properly – three to six months – as these fish suffer when placed in a newly setup system. To keep them healthy, remember to carry out regular water changes.

Ideal conditions

Water: Neutral to slightly acidic, slightly hard.
Temperature: 77-82°F (25-28°C).
Food: Small live or frozen aquatic invertebrates, such as daphnia, mosquito larvae, and bloodworm. Tablet foods and flake food (once it has fallen to the bottom).
Minimum number in the aquarium: 6.
Minimum tank size: 24 in (60 cm).
Tank region: Bottom to midwater.

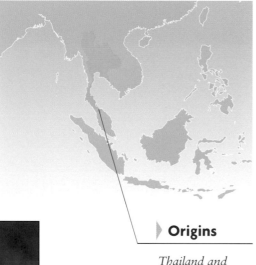

> ▶ **Origins**

Thailand and northern Malaysia.

▶ *Breeding*

There are no obvious sexual differences, and there is no available breeding information.

Left: *Botia have a small spine below the eye (the bifid spine), which they can erect and lower at will as a form of defense. When they use the spine, they sometimes produce an audible clicking sound.*

GOLD ZEBRA LOACH
BOTIA HISTRIONICA
Formerly known as Botia dario, *the gold zebra (or Bengal) loach from India is intensively tank bred in Far Eastern fish farms but rarely spawned in the aquarium. Mature specimens measure 2.5 in (6.5 cm).*

Gold zebra loach

Polkadot loach

POLKADOT LOACH
BOTIA ROSTRATA
This moderately belligerent fish from India and Myanmar (Burma) is also known as the ladder loach. Females are larger and have fewer light blotches – not that these fishes have been successfully spawned in aquariums. Although they belong to the same family as barbs and danios, loaches have evolved to live on the floor of their chosen habitat.

COOLIE LOACH • *Pangio kuhlii*

Coolies are more active at night. They spend the day hidden among plant roots or in nooks and crannies but come out to feed in the early evening when the light starts to fade. If you provide shady areas in the aquarium (use broad-leaved plants) coolies will feel safe and readily come out to feed.

These long, slim fish are very adept at getting beneath undergravel filter plates and up the intake pipes to external filters. There is virtually nothing you can do about this and the fish manage to get out as easily as they got in. Make sure you always use a basket over power filter intakes and, when carrying out a water change, be sure to check what is in the bottom of the filter bucket before you throw out the debris!

Use a fine substrate, as coolies like to bury into it, and coarse gravel can damage their bodies. This burying habit is annoying and can make catching coolies quite a challenge.

Ideal conditions

Water: Slightly hard, slightly acidic.
Temperature: 75-82°F (24-28°C).
Food: Small live or frozen aquatic invertebrates, such as daphnia, mosquito larvae, or bloodworm. Tablet foods and flake food (once it has fallen to the bottom).
Minimum number in the aquarium: 1 (but two are better).
Minimum tank size: 24 in (60 cm).
Tank region: Bottom.

Breeding

Coolies have been bred in captivity. They lay bright green eggs that stick to the leaves, stems, and roots of floating plants.

When catching coolies, try using two nets, one held still against the substrate and the side of the tank, the other to guide the fish along gently.

Size: *Males and females 4.7 in (12 cm)*

Breeding

Since this species tends to spawn in surface plants, include thick plant cover in this area of the aquarium. Use plants that develop a good rootstock below the water surface, such as water lettuce (Pistia stratiotes), instead of plants such as duckweed (Lemna minor).

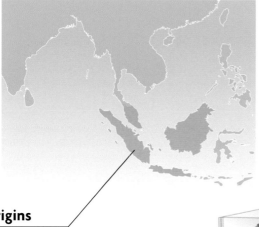

Water lettuce (Pistia stratiotes)

Tank measuring 24x12x12 in (60x30x30 cm).

▶ Origins

Southeast Asia: Malaysia, Singapore, Sumatra, Java, and Borneo.

Set the temperature at 75-80°F (24-27°C).

Soft, acidic water at pH 6.0-6.5.

Include plenty of plants, tubes, and caves for the adults to hide in.

Sex differences

Females fill up with eggs during the breeding season, but otherwise it is almost impossible to sex these fish.

CLOWN LOACH • *Botia macracantha*

It is easy to see why the clown loach is a fishkeeper's favorite, although many do not realize how large these fish can grow. They should be provided with open swimming spaces and plenty of hiding spots; they prefer open holes, so a cave or a piece of bamboo is ideal. A distinguishing characteristic of these fish is a tendency to lie on their sides or in unusual positions. When you first encounter this unusual behavior, it is forgivable to believe that the fish is ill, but it is quite normal. Despite the clown loach's robust and sturdy appearance, it is in fact quite delicate and will only do well in a mature, established aquarium. As with many *Botia* species, the clown loach is sensitive to many aquarium treatments, so always check labels before using any medication. A varied diet is essential to maintain good health and color, and the fish always do best in groups of three or more.

Ideal conditions

Water: Acidic to medium alkaline, Soft to medium.
Temperature: 77-86°F (25-30°C).
Food: Sinking wafers. Feed regularly on frozen foods, such as bloodworm and brine shrimp.
Minimum number in the aquarium: 3
Minimum tank size: 48 in (120 cm).
Tank region: Bottom.

The smooth scaleless skin of the clown loach contributes to its beautiful appearance but also makes the fish more prone to skin parasites.

Size: *Males and females 12 in (30 cm)*

SKUNK LOACH
BOTIA MORLETI

The skunk loach grows to 4 in (10 cm) and gets its common name from the prominent dorsal stripe. It is a good addition to the medium-sized community aquarium, so long as you take care to keep it with suitable tank mates; any small, timid, or slow-moving fish will be harassed. Larger tetras, barbs, and catfishes are good choices. The skunk loach likes to bury, so provide a fine sandy substrate. The aquarium water should be soft and acidic.

▶ Origins

Flowing and still waters in Sumatra and Borneo, Indonesia.

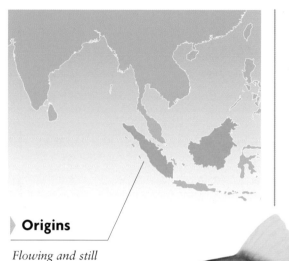

▶ Breeding

Spawning is virtually impossible in the home aquarium. In the wild, breeding occurs only once a year in response to environmental stimuli. The fish breed at the beginning of the rainy season in fast-flowing waters.

The skunk loach is also known as Hora's loach. These fish remain hidden by day but come out at night.

181

CAPE LOPEZ LYRETAIL • *Aphyosemion australe*

Although not often considered for the community aquarium, you can keep these colorful killifish with other small, peaceful species that require similar tank conditions. However, it is best not to combine them with other *Aphyosemion* species because the females of each species can look much the same, and, should you wish to breed them, you will not be able to tell them apart. There is also the possibility that the species may interbreed. Provide plenty of shelter in the aquarium by using fine-leaved plants and one or two floating plants.

The filtration system should provide a very gentle water turnover. These fish cannot tolerate poor quality water, so take care not to overfeed them, as uneaten foods quickly pollute the aquarium.

The brilliantly colored males are popular, but the fish are usually sold in pairs or sometimes trios. Males display ceaselessly to the females. Despite popular myths that they are shortlived, these killifish can live for up to three years.

Ideal conditions

Water: Slightly acidic, soft.
Temperature: 70-75°F (21-24°C).
Food: The fish prefer small live foods, but quickly adapt to the frozen equivalent. Offer flake foods, too.
Minimum number in the aquarium: Pair or trio (1 male, 2 females).
Minimum tank size: 18 in (45 cm).
Tank region: Lower to midwater.

Breeding

The fish hang their eggs by a thread on plants and can be encouraged to use a spawning mop in the aquarium. They produce between 10 and 20 eggs daily. You can remove the mop full of eggs to a separate tank to hatch and add a new mop.

Other fish will quickly nip off the fin extensions unless companions are chosen with care.

Size: Males and females 3.5 in (9 cm)

▶ Origins

Southwest Gabon and Northeast Congo-Brazzaville.

Safety first

Be sure to use a cover glass; these fish jump!

GARDNER'S APHYOSEMION
APHYOSEMION GARDNERI

This is a yellow killifish variety that grows to 2.4 in (6 cm). Males (shown here) are brighter, while females of the various subspecies all look much alike and are a pale tan. These fish fare best in a shaded species tank, and are known as "substrate-spawners," laying their eggs in bottom detritus. A ratio of three females to each male brings the best chance of spawning success.

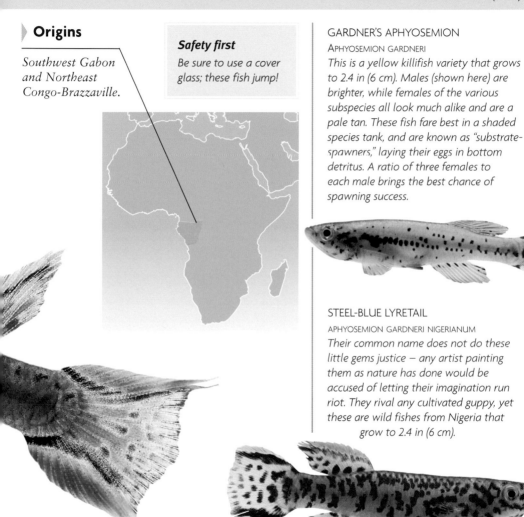

STEEL-BLUE LYRETAIL
APHYOSEMION GARDNERI NIGERIANUM

Their common name does not do these little gems justice – any artist painting them as nature has done would be accused of letting their imagination run riot. They rival any cultivated guppy, yet these are wild fishes from Nigeria that grow to 2.4 in (6 cm).

AMERICAN FLAGFISH • *Jordanella floridae*

These chubby-looking fish are not always seen for sale but are an interesting aquarium fish. Females are fuller in the body and have a dark spot toward the rear of the dorsal fin, while males are slimmer, with stronger patterning. The American flagfish is a good choice for the smaller unheated or cooler aquarium. It is an active lively swimmer and a hardy species ideal for aquarists of all levels. Provide plenty of vegetable foods for this herbivorous fish.

Compatibility

American flagfishes are peaceful toward other tank mates but often vicious toward each other. To control aggression, it is best to keep either a single fish or a group of six or more so that aggression is evenly distributed.

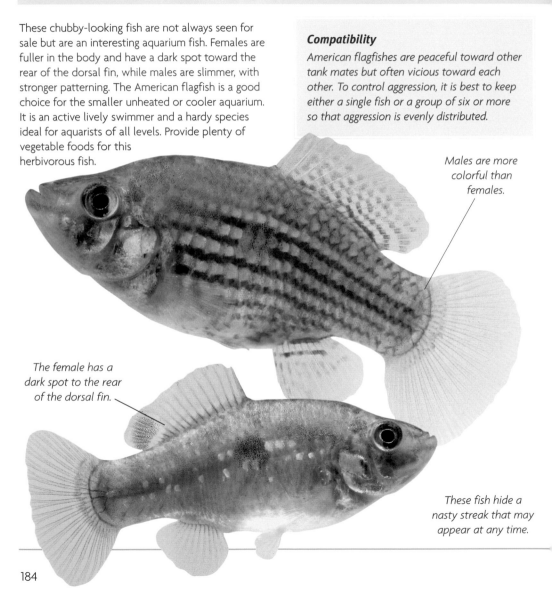

Males are more colorful than females.

The female has a dark spot to the rear of the dorsal fin.

These fish hide a nasty streak that may appear at any time.

Size: Males and females 2.4 in (6 cm)

Breeding

Many aquarists are surprised to learn that some killifishes care for their eggs and young. The American flagfish is one of these. The fish breeds in slightly warmer water among dense plants. Males of this species dig a pit into which the female lays her eggs. During a week or more the adults will produce up to 70 eggs. Unusually, these are then protected by the male (from the female, as well as from other fish) until they have hatched, and the fry are free swimming.

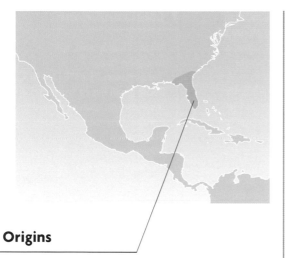

▶ Origins

Florida, particularly the heavily vegetated slow-moving waters in the Ochlocknee and St. Johns River Basins.

▶ *Ideal conditions*

Water: Undemanding; can be kept in slightly brackish water.
Temperature: 64-72°F (18-22°C).
Food: Flake, dried and live or frozen foods. The fish will eat algae.
Minimum number in the aquarium: 1 or 6.
Minimum tank size: 18 in (45 cm).
Tank region: Mainly middle-top.

Temperature 73°F (23°C).

Tank measuring 12x8x8 in (30x20x20 cm).

Soft, neutral to acidic water at pH 6.5-7.

Waterlogged peat substrate as a spawning medium.

BOESMAN'S RAINBOWFISH ● *Melanotaenia boesmani*

One of the larger rainbowfish, *Melanotaenia boesmani*, is an active fish that requires a good-sized aquarium with plenty of open water to swim in. Although it likes clean, clear water, a strong flow is not essential; a gentle current from a power filter will suffice.

When buying these fish, make sure that you acquire both males and females. This is easy to ascertain in adults, as the males have beautiful blue and yellow coloration. It is best to buy young stock and allow them to pair off themselves. Bear in mind that when these fish have been tank bred for several generations, the intensity of color diminishes in each successive generation. Feeding the fish large amounts of live or frozen foods, such as bloodworm, helps to maintain the sheen on the fish.

Ideal conditions

Water: Slightly acid, soft to slightly hard.
Temperature: 75-86°F (24-30°C).
Food: Small live or frozen aquatic invertebrates, such as daphnia, mosquito larvae, and bloodworm. Flake foods.
Minimum number in the aquarium: 4.
Minimum tank size: 36 in (90 cm).
Tank region: Midwater.

Compatibility

Boesman's rainbowfish are quite at home with other fish of a similar size and nature, especially if their companions are not shoaling fish and therefore occupying the same swimming zone in the aquarium.

These are young fish, but when mature, males develop a much deeper body and the head becomes more pointed.

Size: Males 4 in (10 cm), females 3.2 in (8 cm)

▶ Origins

Ajamaru Lakes,
Irian Jaya.

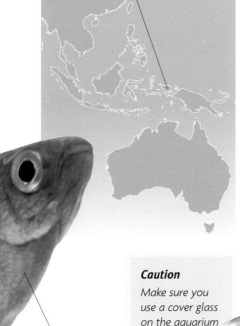

To maintain the
beautiful sheen
on the body, feed
the fish mostly on
live and/or frozen
foods.

Caution
Make sure you
use a cover glass
on the aquarium
as these fish can
sometimes jump.

THREADFIN RAINBOWFISH
IRIATHERINA WERNERI

A unique display of fins give rise to this rainbowfish's common name. In the male, the double dorsal fin has two distinct shapes: the front fin is round and lobe shaped, while the rear fin is tapered and threadlike. The rear dorsal fin is mirrored by an extended anal fin. Both are jet black and extend beyond the red-edged tail. These fin extensions are absent in the females. Being one of the smallest rainbowfish species, the threadfin is suited to any size of display. It occupies the middle and upper layers, where it needs access to dense plant cover. Do not keep it with Siamese fighters or boisterous barbs that will nip the males' extended fins. Maximum adult size: 2 in (5 cm).

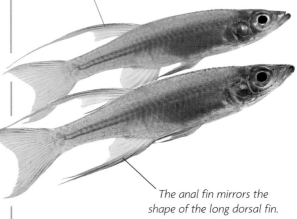

When displaying, these young males
will raise the long dorsal fin like a flag.

The anal fin mirrors the
shape of the long dorsal fin.

RED RAINBOWFISH • *Glossolepis incisus*

The red rainbowfish is a mainstay of the stunningly colored rainbowfish family. The males are bright red and develop a deep body with high fins, while the females remain torpedo shaped, with olive-silver scales. Like many rainbowfish, these are peaceful, active, and easy to keep and breed. As they are active fish, they require plenty of swimming space and similar-sized tank mates. Rainbowfish are often mistakenly overlooked in the aquarium shop as their colors do not develop until the fish have reached a certain size and maturity. Given time, and if kept in a community of similar-sized fishes, the rainbowfish will always "steal the show."

Breeding

The fish will spawn at slightly higher temperatures above a spawning mop or dense vegetation (such as Java moss). Despite its relatively large size, the red rainbowfish produces small eggs. These hatch after about a week, and the small fry are free swimming. Feed them on infusoria as a first food.

Ideal conditions

Water: Neutral to alkaline, medium to hard.
Temperature: 72-75°F (22-24°C).
Food: Live, frozen, and dried foods.
Minimum number in the aquarium: 3.
Minimum tank size: 36 in (90 cm).
Tank region: Middle, top.

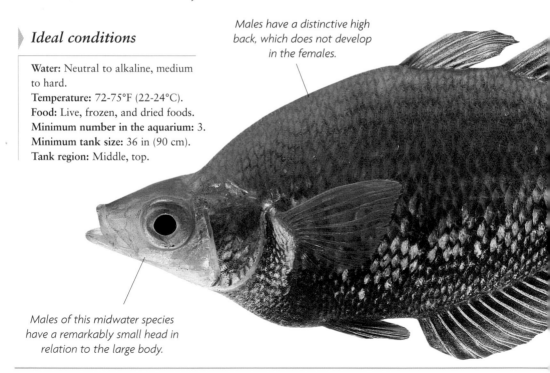

Males have a distinctive high back, which does not develop in the females.

Males of this midwater species have a remarkably small head in relation to the large body.

Size: Males and females 6 in (15 cm)

Origins

New Guinea

The two dorsal fins typical of rainbowfish clearly show up in this species.

WESTERN RAINBOWFISH
MELANOTAENIA SPLENDIDA AUSTRALIS

This vividly colored member of the rainbowfish family does best when housed in a larger display with four or five others of the same species. Like most rainbowfish, it prefers plenty of open swimming space, but otherwise is one of the less demanding species. Feed the fish on a good-quality flake or granular food. Young specimens are a plain silver color, and it may take up to a year for the full colors to develop, but the wait is worth it. The red and blue flanks are a great contrast to other rainbowfish. Males will grow to 4 in (10 cm) and females to 3.2 in (8 cm).

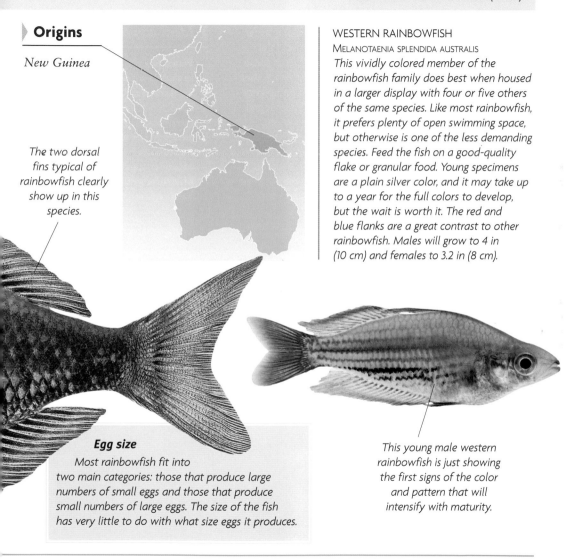

Egg size

Most rainbowfish fit into two main categories: those that produce large numbers of small eggs and those that produce small numbers of large eggs. The size of the fish has very little to do with what size eggs it produces.

This young male western rainbowfish is just showing the first signs of the color and pattern that will intensify with maturity.

DWARF NEON RAINBOWFISH • *Melanotaenia praecox*

This little rainbowfish is a joy to keep. It is undemanding as far as water conditions are concerned, providing you avoid the extremes of hardness and pH. Keep a minimum of six of these peaceful, shoaling fish in the aquarium, but to see them at their best, house 10 or more in a well-planted aquarium with plenty of swimming space. In the wild, they are found in streams and benefit from a gentle flow of water through the aquarium. Ensure that the filtration system is efficient and remember to carry out regular water changes.

Adults are bright blue, which contrasts well with their red fins. To help maintain their coloration, feed them well with live and frozen foods, such as mosquito larvae and bloodworm.

Ideal conditions

Water: Slightly acid, slightly soft to slightly hard.
Temperature: 75-80°F (24-27°C).
Food: Small live or frozen aquatic invertebrates, such as daphnia, mosquito larvae, and bloodworm. Flake foods.
Minimum number in the aquarium: 6.
Minimum tank size: 24 in (60 cm).
Tank region: Midwater.

This beautiful male fish would make ideal breeding stock.

Size: *Males and females 2 in (5 cm)*

▶ Origins

Mamberamo River, northern Irian Jaya, New Guinea.

Rearing the fry

The fry need infusoria or a very fine powdered fry food for a week before they can manage newly hatched brine shrimp and microworms. However, microworms are not a particularly good food for rainbowfishes, because they fall to the bottom and most rainbowfish fry stay very close to the surface.

Breeding setup

Tank: 24x12x12 in (60x30x30 cm).

Include a bubble-up sponge filter.

Slightly hard water at pH 7.5 and 75-79°F (24-26°C).

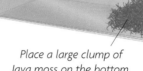

Place a large clump of Java moss on the bottom.

▶ Breeding

Well-fed adults will lay large quantities of eggs over Java moss. If adults remain well nourished, you can leave the eggs and fry in the same tank. However, if you keep other species in the aquarium, remove the eggs, as other fish will quickly polish off the fry. The young do not start to develop their blue coloration until they are about 1 in (2.5 cm) long.

Sex differences

Neon rainbowfish can be sexed very early, as males develop a very deep body shape, a characteristic not normally seen in other rainbowfishes until they are mature.

RAM • *Microgeophagus ramirezi*

The ram, or butterfly, cichlid always catches the fishkeeper's eye with its sparkling jewel-like markings, bright colors, and quirky behavior. Unfortunately, intensive breeding has resulted in a large number of weaker fish being offered for sale. Choosing healthy specimens can be tricky; if you cannot obtain wild fish, then choose a pair and ask your retailer to keep them in a separate tank so you can pick them up later when you are satisfied with their condition. The ram's interesting behavior makes it just that bit different from the usual aquarium stock. Provide the fish with soft water and plenty of little hiding spots among caves, roots, and vegetation. Golden and long-finned varieties are available.

Breeding

If the adults are well fed on live foods, most pairs will spawn within a month of being placed in a breeding tank. During courtship, both fish spread their fins wide and show enhanced colors. The eggs take three days to hatch, but are not free swimming until the seventh day.

Females are smaller and have a reddish belly.

Mature males are slightly bigger with a tall dorsal ray.

Ideal conditions

Water: Acidic to neutral, soft to medium.
Temperature: 75-82°F (24-28°C).
Food: Smaller frozen or live foods, dried foods.
Minimum number in the aquarium: 2.
Minimum tank size: 24 in (60 cm)
Tank region: Middle to top.

Size: *Males and females 2.4 in (6 cm)*

Origins

Orinoco River in
Venezuela and
Colombia.

Choosing breeding stock

When selecting potential breeding stock
in the shop, look at all the fish and watch
how they move around. Fish that have
already paired off will try to stay close
to each other all the time and may even
have staked out a territory.

When both fish are ready to breed, they
usually select and clean a flattish stone
before the female lays a row of about 200
eggs on it. Some pairs prefer to hide from
view and spawn in a cave. Once two fish
have paired off in a breeding tank, remove
the rest to separate quarters.

Compatibility

The fish are
peaceful but will
defend a small area
when breeding.

*Tank measuring
24x12x12 in (60x30x30 cm).*

*Soft, slightly acidic
water (pH 6.5) at
77-82°F (25-28°C).*

*External power filter, with both
intake and return tubes tucked
away at the back.*

Rearing the fry

Compared with most
cichlid fry, these young are
small, but most broods
can tackle microworms
as a first food and can
manage newly hatched
brine shrimp in three days.
After a few weeks, the fry
will be moving well away
from their parents, ready
for life by themselves.

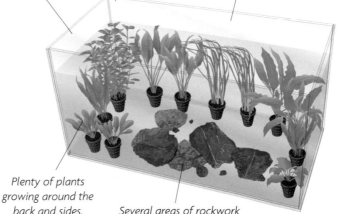

*Plenty of plants
growing around the
back and sides.*

Several areas of rockwork

KEYHOLE CICHLID • *Aequidens maronii*

Keyhole cichlids are delightful, peaceful little fish that adapt well to the community aquarium, where their delicate coloration contrasts well with more flamboyant species. The distinctive "keyhole" marking on each flank is vivid black when the fish is happy, but in stressed fish the color of the flank fades to a dull brown all over. Keyholes also have a black line running through the eye down each flank to the edge of the gill cover.

Their digging is confined to the breeding season and even then they do little damage and do not uproot plants. These cichlids thrive best when kept in pairs and will lovingly care for their fry for a few months before allowing them to fend for themselves. Provide them with sheltered areas where they can hide if they feel threatened.

Ideal conditions

Water: Slightly acid to slightly alkaline, slightly hard.
Temperature: 72-77°F (22-25°C).
Food: Small live or frozen aquatic invertebrates, such as daphnia, mosquito larvae, and bloodworm. Flake foods.
Minimum number in the aquarium: One pair.
Minimum tank size: 24 in (60 cm).
Tank region: Lower to midwater.

Adult males are more colorful and slimmer than females. Their dorsal and anal fins are extended to points.

Breeding

Pairs establish their territory and will raise a family, with both parents tending the fry. When they are ready to spawn, females can be identified by their deeper, rounded bodies. Young fish will not be sexable, so buy three to five to increase the chance of obtaining a pair. A mature pair can produce up to 300 fry, but do not expect to raise all of them. Some will become food for other tank inmates, but quite a proportion will survive and you may need to set up another aquarium to grow them on.

Size: *Males and females 4 in (10 cm)*

▶ Origins

Southern Venezuela and Guyana in slow-moving rivers and streams.

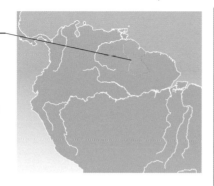

Keyholes have been commercially bred for generations

BORELLI'S DWARF CICHLID

APISTOGRAMMA BORELLI

The flowing fins of this elegant small cichlid often look a bit big for its body! They carry the blue and gold colors from the body and create a wonderful display. The males are half as big again as the females and have pointed dorsal and anal fins. These South American cichlids like to spend time among leaves in the upper layers of the aquarium, so include taller plant species in your display. Maximum adult size: Males 3.2 in (8 cm), females 1.6-2 in (4-5 cm).

A male Borelli's dwarf cichlid proudly displaying in the aquarium.

Size in the wild

In the wild, these fish grow much larger than tank-bred ones, but wild-caught specimens are not often available; when they are, they are much sought after and command high prices.

ANGELFISH • *Pterophyllum scalare*

Angels are majestic fish, beloved of many aquarists. Most commercially available fish are tank bred and many exhibit symptoms of inbreeding, such as poor color and stunted growth, but the most significant factor is the inability of some of these fish to behave normally as cichlid parents. They have no idea what to do with their eggs or fry, and it is generally believed that this is due to the practice of removing the eggs from the parents to hatch and raise the fry separately and thus ensure a much larger brood than normal.

The sexes are not easy to distinguish and the only reliable way is to look at the short breeding tube that extends from the vent. In males, it is pointed, in females, rounded. Buy young fish and grow them up in a planted aquarium. Provide open water in the center, with broad-leaved plants, such as Amazon swordplants, and thickets of vallisneria at the sides and back. If you wish, add some low-growing plants in the center.

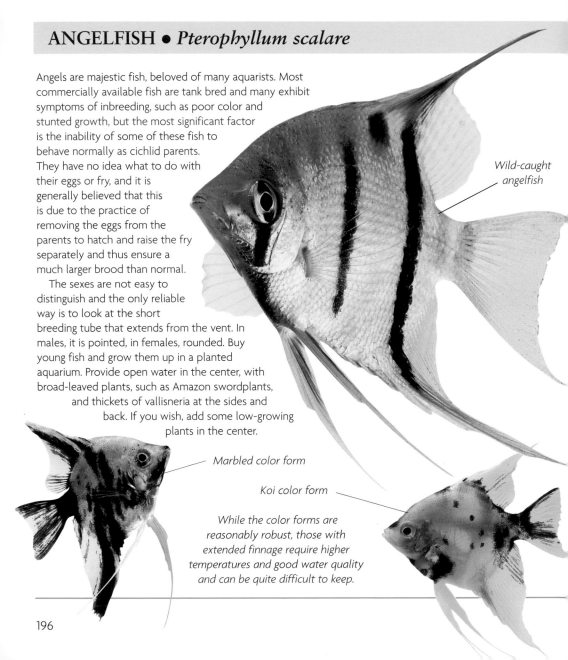

Wild-caught angelfish

Marbled color form

Koi color form

While the color forms are reasonably robust, those with extended finnage require higher temperatures and good water quality and can be quite difficult to keep.

Size: Males and females 6 in (15 cm)

▶ Origins

Central Amazon River and tributaries, into Peru and eastern Ecuador.

▶ *Ideal conditions*

Water: Slightly acidic to neutral, slightly soft to slightly hard.

Temperature: 75-82°F (24-28°C).

Food: Angelfish are greedy and will eat small live foods, frozen and flake foods to excess. This can result in their early demise. Do not overfeed.

Minimum number in the aquarium: 3-4.

Minimum tank size: 36 in (90 cm).

Tank region: Midwater.

Compatibility

Youngsters are peaceful, but as they pair off, angels can become territorial, especially toward other angelfish. At this point, it is a good idea to remove the other angelfish and just keep this pair in the tank. Although they will dominate other species, they do not usually cause any actual bodily harm. Do not keep them with very small fish such as neons, which will be eaten!

ALTUM ANGELFISH
PTEROPHYLLUM ALTUM

These fishes from the Orinoco are much deeper than they are long, and can attain a mature size of 12-15 in (30-38 cm) tall and 6 in (15 cm) long. They have a sharper gradient from head to jawline than ordinary angelfishes. The barred flanks blend cryptically into the underwater habitat of dead wood lit by dappled forest light. They need a larger tank and warmer water than Pt. scalare. These rare fish are highly prized, and if you can get them to spawn (in soft, acid water) you are on to a winner!

Altum angels look fantastic when kept in a shoal.

The deep-bodied altum angels have more vivid markings than their more common cousins.

COCKATOO CICHLID • *Apistogramma cacatuoides*

The cockatoo cichlid is available in a number of color forms, often with intense markings. Males are substantially larger, with extended finnage patterned with red, orange, and yellow, hence the fish's common name. The smaller female contributes just as much to the display, being bright yellow, with a jet black line along each flank. Despite her smaller size, the female can be the more adventurous fish as she moves around the aquarium. Although the fish are territorial, if given enough room in a larger tank, they can become a welcome part of a community aquarium. For the best health and color provide a dark, sandy substrate, plus cave-forming decor, such as bogwood and rocks, and a few patches of vegetation. Keep cockatoo cichlids either in pairs or, preferably, house several females to each male. Avoid keeping them with other cichlids, unless they are in a large aquarium.

Breeding

The female will select and clean a cave site where the eggs and young are heavily defended.

The intense colors of the male are quite different to their wild counterparts but have made the cockatoo cichlid a popular aquarium fish.

The smaller female is attractive if less gaudy than the male.

Ideal conditions

Water: Acidic to slightly alkaline, soft to medium.
Temperature: 72-79°F (22-26°C).
Food: Smaller frozen or live foods, dried foods.
Minimum number in the aquarium: 2.
Minimum tank size: 24 in (60 cm).
Tank region: Bottom, middle.

Size: Males and females 2 in (5 cm)

Origins

Western Amazon Basin in Peru, Ecuador, Southeast Colombia, and Northwest Brazil.

AGASSIZ'S DWARF CICHLID
APISTOGRAMMA AGASSIZII

This small elegant Amazonian cichlid makes up in color for what it lacks in size. Fin coloration is extremely variable. In this example, the flame-red dorsal, anal, and tail fins contrast with the blue flanks. The blue coloration also spreads in a marbled pattern onto each side of the head, making this fish a real gem. Males are generally larger than females and have a more pointed tail. As it is usually quite easy to identify the sexes, these fish are often sold in pairs. However, if they are to breed, you will need to house one male with several females. Being small — 3.2 in (8 cm) — A. agassizii appreciates the cover provided by dense planting and root-shaped pieces of bogwood in the aquarium.

VIEJITA DWARF CICHLID
APISTOGRAMMA VIEJITA

Although not as commonly seen as some other dwarf cichlids, the viejita dwarf cichlid certainly deserves a look-in. In this little South American cichlid species, the male's bright yellow breeding colour is simply stunning. At 3 in (7.5 cm), he is much larger than the female (1.2-1.6 in/3-4 cm), with elongated fins and black spots along the back and flanks. These fish may spawn in your aquarium and will take over a cave in order to do so. They will defend this from other inhabitants in the aquarium but only if they approach too close to the eggs or fry.

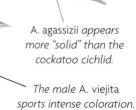

A. agassizii *appears more "solid" than the cockatoo cichlid.*

The male A. viejita *sports intense coloration.*

KRIBENSIS or PURPLE CICHLID • *Pelvicachromis pulcher*

The attractive kribensis is a very good choice for the novice fishkeeper. Wild-caught fish are rarely imported (and expensive when they are), so the commercially raised, tank-bred fish are acclimatized to life in the average community aquarium. When you buy them, watch the tank for a while, and you should be able to distinguish males from females. If you are really lucky, you may even acquire two that have already established a pair bond.

Kribensis will feel at home in a well-planted community aquarium, especially if you provide some caves that can be used as possible spawning sites. For the most part, they are peaceful, and, although they may dig in the substrate, they do not uproot the plants. Make sure you provide a fine substrate to allow for digging, as this activity is an essential part of the breeding ritual for many species of cichlid. They are easy to feed, taking just about anything that will fit into their mouths.

Males are slightly larger, and their dorsal and anal fins are pointed, while the caudal fin has extended rays in the central portion.

The smaller female is also vividly colored and has a bright pink belly when she is ready to spawn. Her fins are rounded compared with those of the male.

200

Size: Males and females 3-4 in (7.5-10 cm)

▶ Origins

Southern Nigeria, mostly west of the River Niger.

Breeding

The krib is an egglayer and typical cave spawner. It is best to grow on six or more youngsters together and allow them to pair off naturally. Alternatively, buy a mature pair. When a pair has settled into their surroundings, the female usually initiates courtship, which can last a month. When ready to spawn, she will select a spawning cave and entice her mate into it. Here, they usually spawn on the roof, laying up to 250 eggs. These take three days to hatch, and the fry become free swimming on the seventh day. Feed the fry brine shrimp and microworms at first, adding fry foods later.

▶ *Ideal conditions*

Water: Slightly acidic, medium hard.
Temperature: 75-77°F (24-25°C).
Food: Small live or frozen aquatic invertebrates, such as daphnia, mosquito larvae, and bloodworm. Flake foods.
Minimum number in the aquarium: One pair.
Minimum tank size: 24 in (60 cm).
Tank region: Bottom to midwater.

Moderately soft, neutral water.

Some areas of plant growth.

Set temperature at 77-80°F (25-27°C).

Tank measuring 24x12x12 in (60x30x30 cm).

Include plenty of rockwork and caves for the pair to choose as breeding sites.

Page numbers in **bold** indicate major entries; *italics* refer to captions, annotations, and panels; plain type indicates other text entries.

FISH INDEX

CREDITS

The publishers would like to thank the following photographers for providing images, credited here by page number and position: (B) Bottom, (T) Top, (C) Center, (BL) Bottom left, etc.

David Allison: 82(T), 169

Aqua Press (M-P & C Piednoir): 82(B), 84, 85, 92, 95, 102(B), 105(L), 109, 116, 120, 130, 134, 138(T,B), 142(B), 152, 156(T), 157, 162, 178, 195, 200(T,B)

Photomax (Max Gibbs): 64, 70, 94, 96, 98, 100, 106, 107, 126, 169, 176, 190, 194

Mike Sandford: 128, 170

Computer graphics by Phil Holmes and Stuart Watkinson
© Interpet Publishing.

Index compiled by Amanda O'Neill.

Publisher's note